The
Kennedy Family
Scrapbook

Family Scrapbook

Nothing, nothing is better than a good editor:
Bernie Geis, Jessie Crawford, Jean Friedman,
and Marcia Ben-Eli.

Cover photograph of John F. Kennedy and Joseph P. Kennedy, Jr.,
courtesy of Pictorial Parade.

Designed by Marcia Ben-Eli
Copyright © 1978 by Stanley P. Friedman
All rights reserved
Published simultaneously in Canada
Library of Congress catalog card number: 78-59789
ISBN: 0-448-14835-8 (hardcover edition)
        0-448-14845-5 (paperback edition)
First printing 1978

Printed in the United States of America

Contents

We have no other American memory like it. They are fixed in our mind, as the French say. The Kennedy family, like relatives living in the next town, wait to be remembered at any time.

Patrick Kennedy *m.* Bridget Murphy

Thomas Fitzgerald *m.* Rosana Cox

Patrick Joseph Kennedy
m. Mary Hickey

John Francis Fitzgerald
m. Mary Josephine Hannon

Joseph Patrick Kennedy *m.* Rose Elizabeth Fitzgerald

Joseph
Patrick Jr.

John Fitzgerald
m. Jacqueline Bouvier

Rosemary

Kathleen
m. William Hartington

Eunice Mary
m. Robert
Sargent Shriver, Jr.

Caroline Bouvier
John Fitzgerald Jr.
Patrick Bouvier

Robert Sargent Shriver III
Maria Shriver
Timothy Shriver
Mark Kennedy Shriver
Anthony Paul Shriver

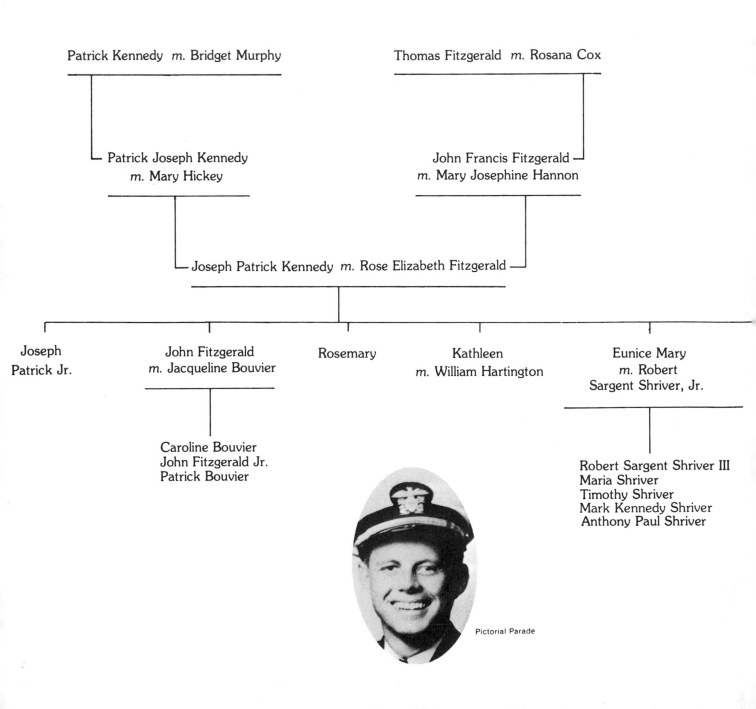

Patricia
m. Peter Lawford

Christopher Lawford
Sydney Lawford
Victoria Lawford
Robin Lawford

Robert Francis
m. Ethel Skakel

Joseph Patrick III
Robert Francis Jr.
David Anthony
Mary Courtney
David LeMoyne
Mary Kerry
Christopher George
Matthew Maxwell Taylor
Douglas Harriman
Rory Elizabeth Katherine

Jean Ann
m. Stephen Edward Smith

Stephen Smith
William Kennedy Smith
Amanda Mary Smith
Kym Maria Smith

Edward Moore
m. Joan Bennett

Kara Anne
Edward Moore Jr.
Patrick Joseph

Kathleen Hartington *m.* David L. Townsend

Meagan Kennedy Townsend

Founding Fathers

They came to America four generations ago, poor and beleaguered among millions of immigrants, from an Ireland in famine. Rose Kennedy once said the rise in America of the Kennedy-Fitzgerald family is a saga. Because they have gained wealth and power and are looked up to in admiration, she believes they have a moral responsibility to make a better world for others.

She also hopes her twenty-nine grandchildren, the fifth generation and her Kennedy heirs, will understand one day that the United States was one of the few places, perhaps the only place in the world, where it could have happened.

A saga, in her words, describes their family story exactly.

Fly over the ocean to County Wexford in south-

In October 1914, Joe and Rose married in a quiet ceremony attended only by family and close friends at the chapel of Cardinal O'Connell. They honeymooned at Greenbrier, West Virginia, for two weeks.

eastern Ireland and you will meet many more Kennedys and Fitzgeralds, descendants with Rose and her American grandchildren of two of Ireland's most prominent and most numerous families. They too became public families with the late President's rise and especially from the days of his spectacular visit. The country, so to speak, had to wait one hundred and twenty years for one man's return, deputy for the millions who left for America.

John Kennedy said that if his great-grandfather had not left the town of New Ross, he might just be working over there in the fertilizer plant or tending bar. But he told the Irish people that though he spent his life in America, it was both as Irishman and American. The citizens of Ireland knew that before he came. Hadn't *they* sent their kin to America? And wasn't it always the point that you cannot undo Ireland from your past?

The decade of the 1840s is a bleak period in Irish history. Absentee landlordism and a growing Irish population worsened the land question. Midway through the decade, a famine struck Ireland. Of its 8.5 million people, over 4.0 million depended on the lowly potato for life and sustenance. "God bless it," said one housewife, "we had only to throw a few of them in the hot ashes and then turn them, and we had our supper." But the potato proved vulnerable to the ravages of the potato blight. In the terrible years after 1845, blight struck repeatedly, continuing into the 1850s. It brought the end of an era in Ireland. Panic and dread were followed by resignation and despair. Starving people wandered around the country begging, many of them dying on the roadways. Typhus wiped out entire families in a month. Cemeteries became overcrowded, and many of the dead had to be buried in communal lime pits. Between 1846 and 1851, a million men, women, and children died of starvation and its attendant diseases. Another one and one-half million decided to leave the stricken country, and most of them, like troubled generations the world over, looked to America.

Meanwhile, Boston needed cheap labor, and the Cunard shipping line wanted ocean traffic to that port. Cunard lowered its fares and advertised the wonders of America. When the new immigrants landed in Boston, the Irish already made up 24,000 of its 120,000 population. Fifty years later, half of Boston's 450,000 people were either Irish immigrants or descendants of the earlier arrivals.

In the mid-nineteenth century, New Ross, where the Kennedy and Fitzgeralds went to leave Ireland for America,was busier than Dublin. Strangers filled the streets. Emigrants carrying all they owned in one bundle paid from $12 to $20 apiece, a fortune to them at that time, for steerage on a packet ship bound for Boston. In a peak year, 100,000 of them sailed for America.

Pat Kennedy and Tom Fitzgerald never met, but the ocean trip they shared is part of our national memory. The danger and suffering they endured is mythical, a traditional story of historic events. Books describe the Irish experience as one of the cruelest of all immigrant trips to America. It may have equaled the slave trip. The slaves, in fact, were valuable property and as such received minimal food and care. This was not true for the Irish in the ship's hold.

The boats were actually called coffin ships. They were small, crowded, and dangerous. Of the 100,000 immigrants who sailed in a peak year, 38,000 died on board. The ocean is filled with Irishmen, it is said today of the Atlantic.

The six-week voyage westward was spent almost entirely in the hold. Only in good weather were the immigrants allowed on deck. Below decks, a man could not stand without stooping. The law required greedy shipowners to provide food, but the law was not enforced. Each traveler carefully husbanded his own rations. An appeal to the captain meant surrender of all money and possessions.

Water, turned rank, could be gagged down only by adding doses of vinegar to hide the odor. Sometimes water was stored in old wine casks, which made it undrinkable; men, women, and children were condemned to nights and days of torture. Reeking privies turned the atmosphere foul and choking. Disease dogged the fleeing Irish; the hasty medical examinations on the quay allowed the sick to slip aboard with the healthy and sent fever raging through the tightly packed holds. During rough weather, passengers were imprisoned in the dark steerage for days on end. Nerves rubbed raw. Men erupted into murderous fights while women and children watched in terror. And single women were preyed upon by rapacious sailors.

In Boston itself, life for the newcomers was best in the streets and pubs. Fish peddlers with tin horns sold fresh cod, mackerel, and haddock. For twenty cents one could buy enough fish to provide for a family of eight, a family size that was not uncommon. Oystermen carried sacks on their backs. "Oys! Buy any oys!" they called. It was a picturesque world of street hawkers and clattering horse-drawn wagons whose drivers sold coal, ice, kindling bundles, fruits and vegetables right off the back of their vehicles. The air was filled with cries and chants and calling out to people upstairs in the tenements. Little chimney sweeps going through the streets called out for work. Peddlers with pushcarts loaded down with crabs and pyramids of oranges, roast peanuts, and raw fish passed through.

But life for the Irish seems to have been harder in Boston than in other cities, even worse than in the New York tenements. Greenhorns were often cheated by sweatshop employers who paid a dollar a day for fourteen hour's work. The exhausted newcomers were bewildered by exorbitant food prices and rents that kept going up. Crowded tenements might house as many as thirty in a room, at a dollar a week in advance. One outhouse served dozens. Filth and garbage rotted in narrow alleys, causing periodic epidemics of cholera, typhus, and tuberculosis. Sometimes wife, husband, sisters,

and brothers slept in the same bed. It was a brutalizing and degrading life. And there was a sense of hopelessness, fostered in part by ignorance. For one cannot forget that the ruling British in Ireland forbade the education of the Irish. Few of the immigrants could read and write.

Patrick Kennedy married Bridgit Murphy in Boston around the half century, and they had four children. One of them was Patrick Joseph Kennedy, who became prominent in Boston politics. He was Joe Kennedy's dad.

Tom Fitzgerald married Rosana Cox in Boston, also around the same period, and they had seven children. One of them was John Fitzgerald, who became mayor of Boston. He was Rose Kennedy's father.

The first generation born in America seems to get ahead much more quickly than their immigrant parents. Unencumbered by the old country's culture, they do not have as difficult an adjustment as their parents endured. And the Irish, compared to the German, Italian, Russian, Swedish, Jewish, and other immigrants, had one advantage. They

The Kennedy homestead near Duganstown, County Wexford, Ireland, belonged to Patrick Kennedy, Jack's great-grandfather, who immigrated to America in 1849.

spoke the language of the country. So they became policemen and firemen, public servants, and wherever they were permitted to do so, entered politics in the early days.

Patrick ("P.J.") Kennedy and John ("Honey Fitz") Fitzgerald saw two of their children, Joe and Rose, married on October 7, 1914, in Boston. But the fathers of the young couple were not on friendly terms. In the Boston coliseum of politics it was a classic Montague versus Capulet. Boston politics was a business of importance rivaled only by food, housing, and possibly sex. It was, after all, the politicians who gave out patronage and jobs. The two men backed opposing factions. And they were very different men—one voluble, one silent; but both were determined, self-made, and of stern purpose.

Honey Fitz had to be father and mother to his

Patrick ("P.J.") Kennedy, Joe's father, was born in an East Boston slum in 1857 and rose through the saloon and wholesale whiskey business to become a Boston political power. He died at age seventy-two in 1929. Joe Kennedy's mother, Mary Hickey (right) was thirty when she married Patrick Kennedy in Boston in 1887. She died in 1923 at the age of sixty-six.

Bundled in fall finery and gloves (left to right), Agnes (six), Tom (three), and Rose Fitzgerald (eight), pose in a photographer's studio for a family portrait. The girls wear twin fur-trimmed coats.

Above: *Rose's parents, the flam-boyant John ("Honey Fitz") Fitzgerald, three times mayor of Boston, and Mary Josephine Hannon. They were married for sixty-one years.*

Mayor Honey Fitz, standing in the touring car, doffs his top hat to present a sterling silver bat to Honus Wagner, sometimes called the greatest ballplayer who has ever lived.

brothers after their parents died. He had the care of six brothers, often having to wash and dress them before sending them off to school. He also washed dishes, made beds, scrubbed floors, sifted ashes, and carried the coal and firewood up three flights to their flat. In addition, he had to go out and earn money to keep the family together.

He was a vibrant person and, once met, an unforgettable one. On his part, he could remember the name of anyone important enough to vote. He could talk to a man for ten minutes at the rate of two hundred words a minute without letting the fellow cut in more than two or three times; and then he'd pat him on the back and tell him how much he had enjoyed the conversation.

He met Josephine Mary Hannon for the first time when she was washing dishes in her kitchen. He

Rose Elizabeth Fitzgerald, in 1906 at the age of fifteen, was the youngest student ever to graduate from Dorchester High School. She is handed her diploma by her father, the mayor of Boston.

was fifteen and she was thirteen. She had soft brown hair, blue eyes, a peach-blown complexion, and a slender figure. After that first meeting, they saw each other often. Eleven years later, they had a church wedding and moved into his home in Boston's North End. Rose Fitzgerald, the second of their children, was born three years after they were married. Five years later, Honey Fitz was elected a U.S. congressman, an office he held for two terms.

He became a famous politician and public character in Boston, eventually more famous as mayor than as congressman. In all his life he never stopped gathering votes. He was never home, days or evenings, except on Sundays for church and rest. He adored politics, and he took his favorite daughter, Rose, not his wife, on his political rounds. Rose learned the game from her father, sometimes attending three and four kinds of social gatherings in a single night. Thirty years later, she knew as much about politics as any of the Irish specialists who were engaged to teach her son John the ropes when he first ran for Congress.

Patrick (P.J) Kennedy was a quiet man. He courted Mary Hickey and married her when he was twenty eight, in 1887. His first son, Joseph Patrick Kennedy, was born in 1889. P.J. was a barkeep who liked to listen. He was determined to get ahead, especially after his father, exhausted by hard work, died at thirty-five. P.J.'s way was to save—after first giving his mother money from his wages—and to go into the saloon business in East Boston's Haymarket Square. He prospered and opened two more saloons.

Politics grew in Boston because the Irish vote grew with large families, and increased with the lowering death rate. P.J., as saloonkeeper, came naturally to politics. He knew office seekers and their supporters, and he gave advice as a successful businessman. He became a Massachusetts state representative and later a state senator. But he did not like campaigning. Functioning as a power behind the throne was more his style.

Joe Kennedy and Rose Fitzgerald met as children at Old Orchard Beach in Maine, where Irish Catholic families in Boston politics went for a week or two each summer. Years after, on another visit to Orchard Beach, they became friends and sweethearts.

Joe Kennedy, as Rose remembers him, was tall, thin, and freckled; he had blue eyes and sandy red-

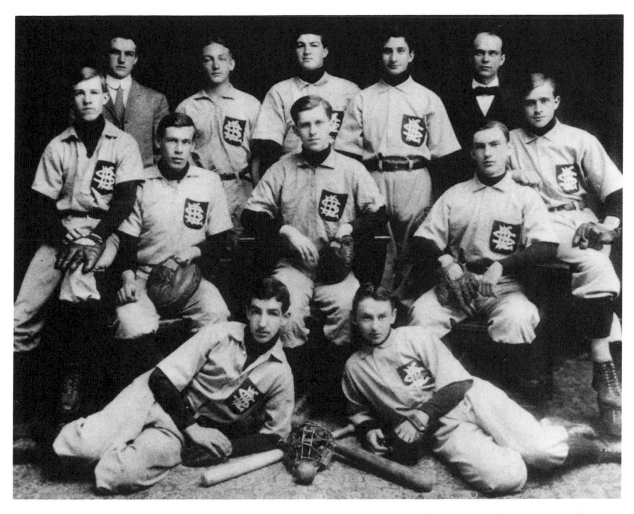

Joe (third from left, middle row), circa 1903, attended Boston Latin, one of the best prep schools in the country. He was captain of the baseball team for two years, loved the sport, and could remember games in detail all his life.

gold hair. His face was open and expressive. Rose thought he had a youthful dignity, which to her conveyed self-reliance, self-respect, and self-discipline. And Rose, according to her sister, was pink-cheeked with coal black hair, clear skin, and blue eyes. She had a fine figure and was enormously vivacious.

When Joe asked Rose to the first dance of the season at Boston Latin School, her father refused to let her go. At home, as in politics, Honey Fitz was "The Little Napoleon." He knew Joe and the Kennedy family well; it was a no-risk afternoon dance that could in no way threaten her reputation; Rose was familiar at getting about Boston alone; and the locale was Joe's conservative school—but his answer was still no.

Next chance for the young people to meet came in the spring at the Dorchester High School graduation dance. Rose invited Joe Kennedy, but quietly and on the sly. Thereafter, they began an

intrigue. In any case, in those days there was no such thing as a formal date or going steady before engagement. They would meet at tennis matches, parties, the library, and lectures. At friends' houses they would help push back the parlor furniture, make lemonade and cookies, and sing and dance to the piano. Joe Kennedy was reputed to be some dancer. Daddy's chauffeur, a co-conspirator, sometimes took the roundabout route home, and to the pleasant surprise of his passenger, Rose, would happen upon Joe Kennedy waiting for a trolley. Nothing to do but stop for a half-hour visit.

Rose couldn't fool her father for long. He, meanwhile, had had frequent fallings out with P.J.

Rose, as a debutante, had a celebrated coming-out party that made Boston front page news.

And as a mayor, he considered the Fitzgeralds a cut above the saloon-keeping Kennedys. Father sent Rose away to France for a year, then on to school at Blumenthal on the Prussian border. After that she went to Manhattanville for a year. The object was for her to forget Joe. But they kept in touch by mail. When Honey Fitz got wind of what was going on, he took more action, in the form of visits for Rose to Europe, Central America, Palm Beach, Kansas City, St. Louis, Chicago, and Baltimore. She met eligible bachelors everywhere.

Joe, meanwhile, went to Harvard. Few Irishmen in Boston at that time could afford college, but if they went at all, it was to a Jesuit school or to Holy Cross. Kennedy went to Harvard, on his own ambitions and those of his strong-willed father. Harvard in those days rated students according to the family's social standing: how old was the money in the family (the older the better) and who was the prospective student's grandfather? An immigrant's son was sure to be an outsider, and he remained one because of religious suspicions on both sides. Joe did not make the best clubs. But he got himself educated in music, history, and science. He had, as he admitted in later years, an inordinate ambition and was a hard, hard competitor. He was also

Harvard graduate Joe Kennedy, without his round glasses, sits at his rolltop desk in his Columbia Trust office. At twenty-five he was the youngest bank president ever known in Massachusetts.

sensitive to criticism all his life and found it hard to take. In college, he pursued prestige and ingratiated himself with the right people.

On graduation, Joe Kennedy became a bank examiner, thus apprenticing himself to the banking trade, but from the inside, where one learns the tricks of that trade. His career choice was to lead to his rise, a national record, and his marriage. His father had money in Columbia Trust, a small East Boston bank. A bigger bank tried to take it over.

The father called on the son for help, and the son became father to the father. Joe went out and borrowed money, bought up the stock, and outmaneuvered his competitor; he kept the stock and became at twenty-five the youngest bank president in America.

Honey Fitz, dazzled by the footwork, suddenly saw Joe Kennedy as eminently eligible for his daughter's hand. He announced the engagement, but almost changed his mind when Joe, needling the old man, got him to pay for a dinner he'd come to for free. Calling it off was academic, however. Rose, as determined by then as Honey Fitz or any Kennedy, had made up her mind. They would marry.

Growing Up

An American life together, starting with their marriage in 1914, opens for Joe and Rose at 83 Beale Street in a seven-room frame house with a white porch. Brookline is twenty-five minutes by trolley from Boston, but a good distance in wealth from the family's poor beginnings.

Twenty-four years will pass as prologue. There are many years ahead for the Kennedys. Their marriage will bring, by inventory: nine children; six houses, each larger and grander; $225 million; high politics; triumphs but also grave disappointments. It will close on a glittering title—Mr. Ambassador—and will bring the ambassador's family to England.

Life in the Beale street house, purchased on a $6000 mortgage for $2000 down, reflected the sweet days of discovery. Rose and Joe, aged twenty-four and twenty-six, had honeymooned for three weeks at the Greenbrier Hotel in White Sulphur Springs, West Virginia. Returning to their

A classic 1919 studio portrait taken during the early Brookline years. Joe Jr., aged four (left), and Jack, two, have the popular Dutch bob haircuts. Rose holds the baby, Kathleen, who is without her booties.

Beale Street house, they had the pleasure of doing things together. In those days, one made one's own fun: concerts, classical readings at Harvard, football Saturdays. . . .

They also loaded themselves up with half a family, four children in five years on Beale Street. Joe Jr. was born in the middle of 1915, Jack in 1917, Rosemary fifteen months later in 1918, and Kathleen in 1920.

Home life was very busy and it was work. To cook, for example, one started from scratch. The first step in making an apple pie was to go down into a dark cellar, bucket in hand, to the coal pile situated at the bottom of the chute in the cellar window and bring up a bucket of coal. You lifted the top stove lid, put in three small shovels full, and then waited three-quarters of an hour before you opened the oven door. Using your apron to protect your hand on the hot oven handle, you put your face down to feel the heat, to judge if the oven was the correct temperature for baking. Meanwhile, you peeled your apples and took the flour can down from the shaft for the dough making. America had fifty years to go before "remove from refrigerator, heat and serve in twenty minutes."

Babies, like Joe, Jack, Rosemary, and Kathleen, were born in bed at home. When the contractions

20

started, the bed was pushed to the sunniest window for good light. Next, the doctor arrived, accompanied by an assistant carrying the ether. Housemaid and nursemaid brought fresh sheets, towels, icebags, and pots and kettles of hot water off the coal stove.

Rose Kennedy, like many mothers in those days, remembers placing her faith in God and following the directions of her doctor. Discomfort was to be expected; happiness would come when she held her child in her arms. Rose recalls the thrill of the birth of her first child, Joseph Patrick Kennedy, Jr., but maintains, "I cherished all of them equally."

For years, life at the house with its many kids resembled a big-city political ward. The mayor, Joe Sr., was often away at his duties, unseen but a strong presence felt, during the years of making money or helping run the government. Rose, the ward boss, managed the nine constituents who grew up and demanded services, attention, favors, and care. The maids, servants, and chauffeur were municipal workers.

It was never a hard life. They never wanted for anything. Which is not to say that life was not difficult, frustrating, lonely, sometimes unrewarding, tragic, worrisome, or depressing. Every family bears up to these things. Religion was a center support, especially for Rose, who went to Mass every morning. She still does.

One day, Joe drove up to the house on Beale Street in a brand new Model-T toot-toot Ford, their first car. Prestigious and a beauty. (Later they switched to a Rolls-Royce.) Well, they wanted a car. There were not that many cars around. Mostly people had to take the trolley. After supper, in the summer's twilight, they went off for a drive over to Coolidge's Corner, where people shopped. A couple of workmen had dug a ditch and put out warning lanterns. By the time they saw the lanterns, it was too late. The new car landed in the ditch. It was an inauspicious beginning to their motoring days. Despite some bruises, nobody was really hurt, and the incident is a hilarious memory of Beale Street days together.

Rose's head spun trying to keep track of her

Rose holds Eunice on her lap, while Kathleen stands beside her at their second Brookline home, on Naples Road. Jack, on the kiddie car, and Joe wear sailor suits that portend days to come. Rosemary, with a beautiful giant hair ribbon, sits on the grass.

many children's vital information. In desperation she finally bought a supply of file cards and index tabs. The cards were to become a Kennedy family legend; people found the logic amusing and charming. What better way to keep track of vital statistics? Almost like a census of the Beale Street, and later Naples Street, wards. The cards for the nine kids recorded date and place of birth, church of baptism, names of godparents, dates of first communion and confirmation; plus records of vaccination, weight, eye exams, Schick tests for diptheria, diseases and their aftereffects, doctors' names, and so on. Although initially an act of desperation, they did provide an extremely useful record. Years later, the cards became an international wonder. When they lived in England, the British press learned about the family institution. They marveled at the cards as one more example of the vaunted American assembly-line efficiency.

Children grow, causing houses to shrink. In 1920, the Kennedys moved to a more fashionable address on Naples Road. (The Beale Street house today is a national shrine.) The new house had twelve rooms with high ceilings; it also had a formal parlor. Here Eunice was born in 1921, Patricia in 1924, and Bobby in 1925. The house had a large porch, so Rose divided it up and put all the children in close age categories in separate sections to play.

By now Joe was rich. The family had nurses, maids, and a British chauffeur named Paris who tooled about in the Rolls. Summers they would travel to Cohasset on Cape Cod, not far from Hyannis. The Kennedys had risen in America, by class and notoriety from Joe's business dealings. But in Cohasset some of Boston's oldest society families also passed the summer. They did not particularly like the Irish or *nouveau riche*. When Joe applied for membership in the local country club, he met the classic American rebuff—the blackball. People who traded in business with him would not associate with him socially.

Not long after, Joe Kennedy put his family aboard a private railroad car and left Massachusetts for New York. The Kennedys now lived in a new, big house in Riverdale, a section of New York City. It was easily within commuting distance from the city. Boston was no place to bring up Catholic children, said J.P. Nor was it a place for a man with still larger money ambitions. In Riverdale, Jean and Teddy, the last of the Kennedy children,

were born, in 1928 and 1932.

When Joe Kennedy was twenty-six, he vowed to make a million dollars by this thirty-fifth birthday. He had less than ten years to do it, but he was in a hurry. One day he met a man named Currie who asked him to help run Bethlehem Steel's shipyard in Quincy, Mass. Joe accepted the proposition, giving over his bank, Columbia Trust, to his father to manage, and he learned the shipbuilding business in wartime. Years later this would help him in politics and he would be named by President Franklin D. Roosevelt to run the Maritime Service.

J.P. earned $20,000 a year plus bonuses at the shipyard. He worked hard and got ulcers. When peace came and shipbuilding collapsed, he went into selling stocks. This too put him in good stead. In 1934, President Roosevelt appointed him head of the Securities and Exchange Commission. In learning the stock game, he made and lost money, but as the years went by, he made far more than he lost. Money came to Joe Kennedy because, as was rightly said, he was a shrewd, tough, ruthless businessman and a sharp dealer who could take your shirt and buttons. He was basically a lone wolf; in fact, the only "partner" he ever had was his family. In the end, all he did, good and bad, wise and foolish, was for the family and the Kennedy name.

Kennedy went into the movie business because he thought he cold outmogul the studio heads. It was J.P.'s forte, a speculators' business, without system, offering endless possibilities. He later put his movie connections to good use too, in the political campaigns of his offspring, who used movie people to entertain constituents and influence voting. Nothing was wasted.

Gathering about him a group of trusted lieutenants, Joe Kennedy went to Hollywood and made movies in a billion-dollar industry, becoming the country's fourth-largest movie producer. Joe acted more like a film magnate than a bank president. He used profanity, a quick grin, and direct speech. He produced cornball dramas, B films for $30,000 apiece; and he consistently made money.

But living in California cut deeply into Kennedy's home life, and he sorely missed his family. Once, years before, he had missed the birth of Patricia by a month while he was working eighteen hours a day on a big deal. Now he lived 3000 miles across the country in a large, rented house on Rodeo Drive in

Beverly Hills. Weeks went by without his seeing Rose and the kids.

When he did get home, he decided that the Riverdale house was no longer big enough for the family. He bought a new and bigger house for a quarter of a million dollars in Bronxville, a prosperous suburb. It was elegant and it was roomy. The kids played baseball on the front lawn and showed movies in their private screening room in the basement. J.P. discovered that Joe Jr., his favorite, was a top student. Jack was the classic family case; bright and talented, he was doing mediocre work and was an atrocious speller.

The children attended dozens of schools over the years. Rose wanted them in private Catholic schools. But Joe wanted a secular education for his youngsters. Joe found nothing wrong with Catholic schools, but he felt the boys would need the broadening influences of the non-Catholic schools. The compromise? The girls went to Catholic

Bobby paddles kid sister Jean around with the skill of a veteran in his pontoon boat at Hyannis.

schools, the boys to secular institutions.

The two older sons were separated. Joe Jr. went to Choate, a prep school in Wallingford, Connecticut. Jack at thirteen actually went to a Catholic prep school, Canterbury, in New Milford, Connecticut. Jack was lonely at school and did poor work. He went out for sports, but couldn't make the first team, an ignominy in a family zealous for sports. When he came down with appendicitis, he was taken out of school. Next fall he too went to Choate.

The girls went to Catholic schools, then on to a Catholic college, Manhattanville, at Purchase, New York.

Rose bore the day-to-day responsibilites of raising the family. Strong and self-sufficient, she bore up under the husband's long absences as her

Jack, eight, in his knicker days at Dexter School in Brookline.

Getting the hang of it, two novice skaters, Teddy (seven), and Jean (ten), hold firmly to Rose's hand on an icy mountain lake in St. Moritz, Switzerland.

Right: Kathleen in derby, checked coat, and twill jodhpurs shows handsome young Bobby the way on famed Rotten Row, where kings, dukes, and princesses ride.

A laughing summer's day at Hyannis Port. Left to right: Bobby, Jack, Eunice, Jean on daddy's lap, Rose in cloche hat, Pat sans front teeth, Kathleen, Joe Jr., and Rosemary. The terrier, observing all, is Buddy.

Joe and Rose's first house, at 83 Beale Street, Brookline, Massachusetts, where Jack, Joe Jr., Rosemary, and Kathleen were born, is now federally owned.

In 1934, Joe and Rose had been married for twenty years. Joe headed the Securities and Exchange Commission under the Roosevelt administration.

mother had done with Honey Fitz. Rose considered her marriage one in which work was shared. Joe handled business decisions, she handled family discipline. Jack was later to say that his mother was the glue that held the Kennedys together.

During this period Rose instituted the now famous table discussions—on current events, people, religion, values. Money was never discussed. But those table discussions, never trivial, were extremely important. Rose believed that children should be encouraged to have ideas and speak up for them, with no fear of ridicule. She had rules. Promptness to dinner, brushing teeth after every meal, no smoking, no drinking, pick up

your clothes, read books for the mind and stories clipped from newspapers for discussions at table. Some of the rules were adhered to by the kids, others were often broken. She did the spanking. She used a ruler on the hand or behind, but often it was a coat hanger, an object that is now part of the family lore. Years later, when Eunice was having her fifth child, Rose went down to help with her four grandchildren and found that her reputation had preceded her. Eunice's boys had removed all the coat hangers in the house and put them down the laundry chute.

It fell to Joe Jr., the eldest, to become the surrogate father. Seven of the children hero-worshipped Joe, the bright one, the athlete, the know-all. But, for Jack, he was tough competition. They fought regularly and hard, as only brothers can.

In 1930 Joe Sr. went to the New York governor's mansion to see Franklin Roosevelt, his old

Eunice, the image of a model in print shorts; Bobby, an adolescent sixteen with his wild sports shirt; chunky Teddy, nine; Jean, thirteen and somber in saddle shoes pose during a tennis session on the front court at the Palm Beach home.

Below: Jack, on his 1939 summer vacation from Harvard, and Bobby watch from an upper balcony of the embassy as riders pass in the street below during the changing of the Buckingham Palace guard.

Left: A wholesome-looking Teddy, nine, plays monkey-man in a palm at the Kennedy Florida home.

Farewell America, hello London. On the deck of the liner Manhattan *in New York, February 1938, Joe Kennedy readies to sail to England as the new U.S. ambassador. Seeing daddy off are (left to right) Pat, Kathleen, Eunice, Robert, Jean, Teddy, Rosemary, and Joe Jr. Rose, recovering in Florida from an appendix operation, will join Joe with the children six weeks later.*

acquaintance from shipbuilding days. Roosevelt, once assistant secretary of the Navy and representing the government, had bargained and fought bitterly with Joe, representing the shipyard. Now Roosevelt wanted to be the next president and he wanted Joe's help.

Roosevelt found an ally. "I wanted Roosevelt in the White House for my own security and the kids'. I was ready to do anything to elect him," said Joe. It was the time of the Great Depression. Capitalism needed rescuing. Roosevelt would bring reforms.

And Kennedy thought Roosevelt was a winner.

Franklin D. Roosevelt and Joseph P. Kennedy were alike. Family men, but with one noted difference. The success of the children in the Roosevelt family was individual; Kennedy success was collective. One Kennedy carried the next, as they were taught to do. And their father's will shaped the family as a whole.

Kennedy gave Roosevelt $25,000, lent the Democratic party $50,000, and raised $100,000 in campaign contributions. In today's dollars, that would be eight times as much money. Kennedy also helped swing William Randolph Hearst's crucial convention votes to Roosevelt, who got the nomination. Joe traveled with FDR on his campaign train as an adviser.

When Roosevelt reached the White House he made Joe head of the SEC, a very important job. Before he took over that job, Joe befriended the

President's son, Jimmy, Roosevelt's most influential confidant. They went to England, where Jimmy helped Joe jump the gun on the coming repeal of Prohibition by getting him an English liquor franchise. The liquor was stockpiled in America as "medicinal." Joe made a killing.

Kennedy, now SEC head, came to Washington with his long-trusted lieutenant Edward Moore (Teddy was named for him). Joe Kennedy rented a twenty-five-room house in Marwood, near Washington. The Hindenberg palace, Joe called it. But it was the only house he could find that was big enough to accommodate all his family when they came for Washington visits.

Roosevelt dropped in often at the Marwood house, for double martinis. They watched the latest movies in the special screening room. Joe was not awed by Roosevelt. He talked to him in blunt language. Mrs. Roosevelt, realizing the President was isolated in his job, encouraged Joe to continue being straightforward and informative. Tell him just what you think, she urged.

When Joe finished his work with the SEC, he wanted to be made Secretary of the Treasury, a cabinet office. Roosevelt thought not. He already had a good treasurer in Henry Morgenthau. He also thought Joe was too independent. FDR knew he would lose control of Treasury if Joe ran it.

FDR gave Joe an impossible job, head of the Maritime Commission. Joe was supposed to pull the ship industry and the unions together into a respectable U.S. Merchant Marine. It couldn't be done; government, shipping, and unions were all in conflict with one another. Only time and history could change things. Joe gave up the job.

In 1937, when Robert Bingham, the American ambassador to England, fell fatally ill and came home, Kennedy asked for the job. He had been told by a friend, "You'll be the most important American in Europe."

Roosevelt wanted an ambassador who knew England's most important people, both in and out of government. Kennedy knew many of the highest-placed Britons from his business days. Roosevelt also needed certain kinds of inside information from Europe; the winds of war were blowing. He felt Kennedy could be trusted to give him the blunt truth, to cut through any face-saving fiction called propaganda. He appointed Kennedy as ambassador.

That Joe was the first Irishman and first Catholic

Eunice and Rose in Brazil at famed Sugarloaf Mountain. Jack flew down to join them after a term at Stanford University in 1941.

ambassador to Great Britain, Ireland's oppressor, was an irony not lost on anyone, especially the English. But they took it well, In fact, the British press fell for Kennedy's colorful style and loved his large and photogenic family. "The highest compliment Roosevelt could pay Great Britain," one newspaper said.

For Joe, the job had psychological rewards that he could never have bought with money. He had prestige and public admiration. For as long as he would live, he would have the classy title of Mr. Ambassador. But this post was to lead to his darkest hour, an episode of rejection and disaster that would lead to an eclipse of the Kennedy name.

The Years Abroad

I n 1938 Joe Kennedy went to live in England. For the next three years he would serve as the American ambassador to the Court of St. James's. Suddenly the Kennedy name became celebrated and fashionable on both sides of the Atlantic. Everybody in the family, including the smallest children, was sought out for interviews.

Public life wasn't a new experience for Rose. Not as a Fitzgerald in the old days. Nor as a Kennedy. But she had never been recognized and photographed with such regularity.

In New York aboard the liner *Washington*, ready to sail to London, she and the children were pursued by the press. The wife of the new ambassador to England was society news. She had six staterooms for the children and a seventh for a nurse and governess. She was sailing with her family to meet her husband, who had preceded her

Three beautiful American ladies on their way to be presented to the King and Queen at court in 1938. Kathleen (left), Rosemary, and Rose in the same dress she would wear twenty-three years later to her son's inaugural ball.

to London by six weeks while she recovered in a Boston hospital from an appendectomy.

"Isn't it a task to shift this whole brood?" She was asked by a reporter.

She told them it wasn't a task because the family moved to Florida twice a year. They were all experts at packing. Trained by her father always to speak positively to the press, she told the newsmen she and her family were happy about the appointment. She added that they were all prepared to represent the best American qualities. The children had boned up on British royalty and its practices. At this point Teddy, aged seven, piped up saying he knew nothing about the king. But he had read about the royal princesses and that's who he wanted to meet.

When they arrived in England and were photographed, a headline described the Kennedys as "Nine Ambassadors." The British public thought this wonderful! They agreed with Rose. All the Kennedys, not just the man in striped pants, represented America.

The papers were filled with their doings. Reporters pursued Rose and wanted to know precisely how old she was. What were her secrets for keeping her marvelous figure? What exercises did she take? And where did she develop that wonderful camera smile? Where did she get all her energy at such a late age? She was nearing her fifties then.

Joe Kennedy also received wide press and radio coverage. He was terrific copy! "The USA Nine-Child Envoy," he was called. "The father of his country," they added.

In his first interview, the man who came to deal in foreign affairs put his feet up on the desk and told reporters candidly that Americans weren't interested in foreign affairs. "Some are probably more interested in how Casey Stengel's Boston Bees are going to do next season."

This blunt American style was appealing to the reserved British. Shortly afterward, Joe had a rare piece of luck playing golf that added a tinge of awe to the British perception of his character. He scored a hole-in-one on his first day out. It made every paper, appearing on the front page of two. Jack and Joe, still at Harvard but commuting to England, needled their old man. "Dubious about hole-in-one," they cabled.

Back home in America, readers followed the Kennedy adventures the way they did the comic strips. They were turning into a topical joke. From Harvard, Jack wrote a letter to London. He'd seen Sophie Tucker and Victor Moore on Broadway in *Leave It to Me*. Sophie appeared as Rose's counterpart, the wife of the ambassador to Russia. But she had only five daughters. Poor lady, with four more she "would have had London." But give them the next five years and she'd catch up. She wouldn't give *that* for the Kennedys! "It's pretty funny, and jokes about us by far got the biggest laughs, whatever that signified," Jack wrote.

Their fame back home prompted a curious research by some inquiring person in government. He came up with the fact that one Andrew White in the Treasury Department had seventeen children. This dispelled the myth that the Kennedys had the most children of anyone in federal service.

The giant six-story house used by the American ambassador fronted on Prince's Gate, with a large garden and lawn in the back. It was a gift of J. P. Morgan. It had eight baths and bedrooms for the Kennedy family, and on the top two floors, thirteen bedrooms and baths for the servants.

The Kennedys reduced the staff, using some of their rooms for guests; they saved two for Joe Jr.'s and Jack's visits to London from Harvard. To cover the bare walls, they borrowed paintings from William Randolph Hearst. They tried turning this cold castle-sized house into a home. The house had an elevator. Bobby and Teddy got to it and made up a "trips into an airplane" game. But Rose put a quick stop to that. It's a machine, not a toy, she reprimanded.

Whatever Rose had to learn about diplomatic protocol, she gained from the British staff of maids and butlers. Two months after her arrival at the embassy, she and Joe had the King and Queen to dinner. As Their Majesties entered, the young Kennedy boys waited in a circle in their navy blue suits; the younger girls in their pretty white dresses joined them. After the royal pair met the adult guests, they passed among the children, warmly greeting each child. The boys bowed stiffly and the girls dropped curtsies. Then, as the adult company went in to dinner, Teddy, Bobby, Jean, and Pat, the four youngest children, dropped out; Joe Jr., Jack, Kathleen, Rosemary, and Eunice went to a special table. Young Teddy, trotting off into retirement, let everyone in hearing distance know how unhappy he was about this. It did him no good. He got sent up with "no ands, ifs, or buts, please."

Next day, reporters asked Rose what she and the queen had talked about. Not politics or Anglo-American relations, Rose answered, but the universal topic—their children. "We left the men at the table and went upstairs. She asked me if I always got up to see the kids off to school. She said she did, but then went back to bed." Rose did not. "I told her I used to get up for the six children, but when seven and eight and nine came, I said to myself, this can go on forever."

The children were put in English schools. A first experience for Eunice was being reprimanded by a princess, who accused Eunice of showing an undignified American crudeness on the playing field. Eunice had learned to express herself with victorious shouts and cries whenever she scored in family competition. One just didn't do that in hockey at Sacred Heart, the princess explained. "Hey! Hey!" was something of a dig against the losing side. Eunice changed her ways.

Jean, who disliked being corrected at age ten, had a nun point out a mistake in arithmetic her first day in school. Jean eyed the problem once more and said indignantly, "Well! Five goes into nine twice in America. I don't see why it doesn't in England!"

Pat, very pretty and wistful at age fourteen, and a

math whiz, was also gifted with acute powers of observation. She wanted to know why English servants were so polite. When she was told they had been trained to act that way, she replied, "Well, somebody should train them out of it because they all look like they hurt inside when they talk to you."

The children had other adjustments to make. The rain was a bit much. The food was unfamiliar. In fact, when they were back in London from school for weekends at the embassy, it was worth the cook's life to serve any English standby such as mutton and cabbage.

Bobby and Teddy thought the language was "funny." But they did pick up and use "jolly," as well as try cricket and soccer in the embassy garden.

Sailing to London from New York to join Joe in England are (left to right) Kathleen, Bobby, Teddy, Jean, Rose, and Pat. The younger Kennedys are squinting in the sun on the ship's top deck.

Bobby, aged thirteen, met princess Elizabeth, the future queen, at a garden party. They got along by talking downhill skiing.

Meanwhile, back at Harvard, the competition between Joe and Jack was no longer overt. Still, Joe was a popular sports figure, and Jack, envious, tried hard to match him. But he failed to make the swimming team as a backstroker. He also turned out for junior varsity football. Small, light and thin,

Flying over to Rome out of London's Croydon Airport on Air France for the coronation of Pope Pius, Jack, looking ambassadorial like his dad, foregoes his aversion to hats and emulates his father in a dapper homburg. Joe Sr. represented President Roosevelt at the 1939 coronation.

Above: *Their Royal Majesties at the American embassy. The now-famous exchange took place that evening between Rose and Queen Elizabeth about the difficulties of getting up in the morning to take care of the children.*

Below: *The family, in the paneled dining hall of the thirty-six-room embassy at 14 Prince's Gate, wait for dinner to be served by members of the staff of twenty people.*

Jack, on a European vacation trip in 1937, shows a little of his dexterity at juggling for the camera.

Right: Joe Jr., successfully dodging the opposition in a rugby team scrimmage, prepares for the Harvard-Cambridge (England) team game in 1938 at Harvard.

Left: *Jack, in tank suit, climbs out of the Harvard pool after a workout. He was after, but missed, a place on the 1938 Harvard swim team.*

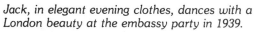

Jack, in elegant evening clothes, dances with a London beauty at the embassy party in 1939.

Winthrop House, Harvard, where Jack lived during his student days, 1937 to 1940.

he went at it very hard. One fall day, he crashed on the frozen ground. He got up slowly. His back was injured. It was the beginning of a trauma that gave him aggravating pain the rest of his life.

In his last year at Harvard, after Joe had graduated, Jack became the scholar his ambitious father knew he could be. He used his intelligence to write an exceptional thesis graded *magna cum laude*. Later it was published as a book, *Why England Slept*, and it sold well in both the United States and England.

The heartache of the Kennedy family was Rosemary, who was retarded. When she was growing up she had responded well to the intense interest of the whole family. She was slow, but she got along. For a time, she was in a special school in Hertfordshire, which helped her. But as she grew older, during the time the Kennedys were in England, she became difficult. She found it harder to concentrate and remember. She developed a temper. There was frustration at being unable or restricted from doing things her sisters and other grown women her age did. She had seizures and rages. She struck out at people. In 1941, after England, Rosemary underwent neurosurgery in America that eliminated the seizures and violence, but left her childlike forever. She was permanently confined in a special home in Wisconsin.

A year of parties, diplomatic work, and socializing passed. Summer and vacation days were coming. Why not travel on the Continent? France was just across the channel. Beyond lay Italy, where Roman Catholicism had its center. Then there was Germany, which Rose knew from her finishing school days. Ireland, too, their ancestral home, could be visited.

And so off to discover the world! By 1939, the phrase "our nine ambassadors" was changed to "join the Kennedys and see the world!" Jean, Teddy, Bobby, Pat, and Rose covered France, Switzerland, and the Netherlands. Joe Jr. went to Czechoslovakia, Poland, Russia, Sweden, Denmark, Berlin, and Paris. Jack and Kathleen took a small car through Austria and parts of Poland. Eunice, Pat, Bobby, and Jean toured Ireland and

On the evening of the King and Queen's first visit to the American embassy, the entire Kennedy family poses for a superb formal portrait. Left to right: Rose, Teddy, Rosemary, Joe Jr., Joe, Eunice, Jean, Jack, Bobby, Pat, and Kathleen.

UPI Photo

Family skiing lessons ("Everybody bend the knees, please.") for Pat, Eunice, Robert, and Joe who wait for Rosemary to follow suit, on a trip to Switzerland.

Scotland. Rosemary caught up with them in Scotland.

Teddy visited St. Moritz and Cannes. But his memorable moment came when he went to Rome for the coronation of Pope Pius XII.

The Kennedy family had a seat of honor at the coronation ceremony. Joe was special American representative to the ceremony. Afterward, they were invited to a private audience with His Holiness. And Teddy had an honor never before given to a young American boy, according to Vatican authorities. Pope Pius, reviewing a 1936 visit to New York when he was Cardinal Pacelli, recalled meeting Teddy at the Kennedy home in Bronxville. Little Teddy had sat on his knee. Now the Pope arranged for him to make his first communion that day in his private chapel in the Vatican. When Teddy emerged, Jean ran up and asked him if he was scared. He said, "Naw. I wasn't

afraid. He patted me on the head."

Throughout their travels, the children were required to go with the people of the country, preferably by bus, and not first class. They were to learn the ways of the people and observe their daily lives. And they should keep diaries so that in later years they would have the pleasure of remembering again their adventures.

But tempering the excitement and adventure was a general uneasiness that said any return visit was not possible in the near future. War was coming. Everybody knew it was coming. You could feel it. The days of pleasure were ending. And the future would come down hard on the Kennedy family in many painful ways. The first change brought Joe Kennedy political bankruptcy.

England was looking to America for involvement if not direct help in the war. Britain was barely prepared to battle a powerful military country like Germany. But Joe Kennedy, at heart an isolationist, wanted America to stay out of the war. He was aware that Roosevelt and the State Department were pursuing the opposite course,

Our American ambassadors, Teddy (left) and Bobby, and a baby elephant who wants more peanuts, officially open the Children's Zoo in London for the season.

Right: *Joe Jr. on a London street corner reads about the serious war threat between Germany and Poland over the Free City of Danzig.*

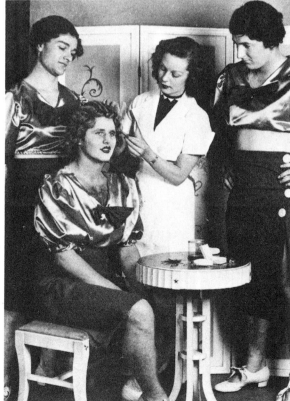

The hairy-legged chorus girl in the chair having his marcelled wig adjusted is Joe Jr. just before a rehearsal of the annual Harvard Pi Eta Club show.

41

involvement. So Kennedy was at odds with his "employer."

Moreover, the situation in England was complicated. Prime Minister Neville Chamberlain tried to appease Hitler to avoid war. Kennedy agreed with and encouraged this policy of giving in to Hitler. A working capitalist, Kennedy believed that if war did come, it would bring radical social and economic changes to America. England's loyal opposition, including Winston Churchill, was against appeasement. They opposed Kennedy and said so openly.

Thus, the most popular American ambassador in Europe since Benjamin Franklin was slowly becoming disliked privately and was later rejected publicly when he spoke his mind. Kennedy's role as ambassador called for diplomacy, which meant using discretion and stifling his ego. That was something he could not really do.

One evening, some time after the Munich Pact made it clear to the allies that handing Czechoslovakia over to Hitler to avoid war had been a futile and pointless waste, Joe addressed the Trafalgar Day dinner guests at the Navy League. Despite the Munich fiasco he still advocated taking a soft line with Hitler. "After all, we have to live together in the same world, whether we like it or not," he said.

Rose had privately warned him, as Joe admitted to his fellow guests, against saying this in public. The speech was considered a diplomatic blunder on both sides of the Atlantic. Kennedy had gone too far.

At home, a political movement had been afoot to make Joe Kennedy a Democratic candidate for the Presidency in the coming election. Roosevelt was not expected to seek a third term. After Joe's speech, the movement was abandoned. It seemed only a matter of time before Joe Kennedy would be recalled.

On September 3, 1939, just two hours after Germany declared war on England, Rose, Joe Jr., and Jack were forced for the first time to seek refuge in an air-raid shelter. Two hours later, they had to scurry back as they emerged from the House of Commons to hear a "war declared" speech. They were carrying gas masks. The time to pack up and return to America was now. Rose prepared, along with many fellow Americans in Britain, to go home.

Joe stayed behind, of course. Joe Jr. and Jack also remained to help repatriate other Americans. Some, rescued from the sinking passenger ship *Athenia* on its way to Canada, needed serious help. Eventually, Joe Jr. and Jack had to leave England, too. Public interest in the Kennedys as society news dwindled.

Meanwhile, Joe Kennedy's antagonist, Winston Churchill, became England's Prime Minister. Churchill worked directly with Roosevelt. He simply by-passed America's ambassador to England.

The spacious embassy was lonely and silent for Joe, with everyone gone home. He wrote discouraging letters while receiving encouragement by mail from his family. But his heart was not in his work. He derived no feeling of accomplishment. In fact, he disliked the job at that point. He thought he was wasting his time.

Finally, in 1940, he decided to fly home by Dixie Clipper. The British gave him a warm sendoff. The King and Queen invited him to Sunday lunch. He was photographed shaking hands with Prime Minister Churchill at 10 Downing Street.

In late February, after the American election, Kennedy resigned as ambassador. The Kennedy name quickly went into eclipse. It represented the prewar era that was no longer important. Another generation would have to find an opportunity to come into its own carrying the Kennedy name.

A cordial farewell outside 10 Downing Street between Prime Minister Churchill and Joe Kennedy, as Joe prepares for his return and resignation in America. An antagonism, which is not evident here, existed between the two men over Anglo-American relations.

The Family Apart

The summer of 1940 found all the Kennedys back in America. It was to be the last time that all eleven of them would be together. As with many families, the tragedy of war would change their lives.

In the fall, Joe Jr. registered at Harvard Law School. He was also elected a delegate to the Democratic National Convention in Chicago. He went supporting Jim Farley against Roosevelt's third term, taking baby political steps toward keeping a vow to become the first Catholic President of the United States. He held out his delegate vote to the very end against Roosevelt. But it was no use. He never avenged his father's bad times with the President.

Months before Pearl Harbor, a peacetime draft law was passed by Congress. Both Jack and Joe Jr. registered. Joe Jr. then volunteered to join the U.S. Navy Air Corps as a cadet.

The handsome navy brothers: Jack, a lieutenant (jg.) and Joe, an ensign, December 1942.

A year later America was at war and Joe Jr. was a commissioned pilot. He was handed his wings on graduation by his father, who made the commencement address. Joe Jr. was not sent to combat as he wanted, however, but spent a year patrolling the Caribbean waters in a slow, cumbersome observation plane, watching for enemy submarines. Jack expected to be called up by the army as soon as he finished Harvard in June of 1941. So he followed Joe's steps. He tried to enlist in the navy but was rejected because of his health. He could have stayed out of the war, but he wanted to get in. He spent several months exercising and eating properly. On his second try the Navy accepted him. He was put on an intelligence desk in Washington. He found that boring. By pulling strings, he got himself reassigned to torpedo-boat school in Milton, Rhode Island.

Two children were in the service now, and a third followed. In June 1943 Kathleen, nicknamed "Kick," gave up her reporter's job in Washington on the *Times Herald*. She went to London and joined the Red Cross, returning to a country where the people and life she had led as an ambassador's daughter were wonderful.

Kick was like Rose. Small, entertaining, and witty, she and Jack and Joe Jr. had been a

Kathleen, working for the American Red Cross during the height of the war, cycles her way around London on a one-speed.

threesome in the family despite the age difference. She looked older than she was, and many thought her the oldest daughter, though she was second after Rosemary. Kick had many friends in London from her old days there. One was William John "Billy" Hartington. He was a titled Englishman, the Marquess of Hartington, and a captain in the Coldstream Guards. There was talk of marriage, but it was a problem. Kick was Catholic and Billy was Church of England.

By now Joe Jr. was in England with Kick, attached to the RAF Coastal Command, flying at night by radar to protect the English coast against German subs.

Meanwhile, Bobby was ready to graduate from his last year of high school at Milton Academy in Massachusetts, one of a dozen or so schools he had attended in as many years. He, too, had passed to draft age. Joe Jr. urged Bobby to join the naval air corps on his eighteenth birthday. Bobby did want to be a pilot. Indeed, when he was seventeen he was bitten by flying when he visited Joe Jr. at the Norfolk air base. Joe Jr. had sneaked Bobby aboard his plane on a search mission and let him fly it from the co-pilot's seat. Bobby signed up for naval air training and was sent to Bates College in Maine for eight months of V-5 schooling.

Jack was in the Pacific by this time, and he wrote Bobby a letter filled with ironic and grudging sentiment, a tone Jack used often with his kid brother both then and later, when Jack was President and Bobby his attorney general.

Dear Robert,
    The folks sent me a clipping of you taking the oath. The sight of you up there, just as a boy, was really moving particularly as a close examination showed that you had my checked London coat on. I'd like to know what the hell I'm doing out here, while you go stroking around in my drape coat, but I suppose that what we are out here for, or so they tell us, is so that our sisters and young brothers will be safe and secure—frankly I don't see it quite that way—at least if you're going to be safe and secure, that's fine with me, but not in my coat brother, not in my coat. In that picture you looked as if you were going to step outside the room, grab your gun, and knock off several of the house-boys before lunch. After reading Dad's letter, I gathered that cold vicious look in your eye was due to the thought of that big blocking back from Groton. I understand that you are going to be there until Feb. 1, which is very nice because it is on the playing fields of Milton and Groton, and maybe Choate, that the seeds will be sown that in later years, and on other fields, will cause you to turn in to sick bay with a bad back or football knee.

    Well, black Robert, give those Grotties hell and keep in contact with your old broken down brother, I just took the physical examination for promotion to full Looie. I coughed hollowly, rolled

Jean in picture hat, white gloves, and carrying two dozen red roses, waits with Joe and Rose to christen the new destroyer U.S.S. Joseph P. Kennedy, Jr. on the pier in the Quincy, Massachusetts, shipyard. Bobby will serve later as a seaman on board the ship named for his brother.

Rose smashes a bottle of champagne over a tanker's bow in Newport News, Virginia, a month after World War II breaks out in Europe. The Esso Richmond will become crucial for shipping fuel during the war.

Right: *Jack, shirtless, in sunglasses and ball cap, poses (right) on the still-intact* PT-109 *with his enlisted crew in the Solomon Islands.*

The war hero sports a cigar, a lifetime indulgence, and rests in his navy dungarees under the Palm Beach sun in 1945, just before his medical discharge.

Right: *The leaders of the PT crews horsing around on the front steps of their officer's quarters in the Solomons in 1943. Left to right: Jim Reed, Barney Ross, "Shafty" Kennedy (as Jack was nicknamed), and Red Fay in front "riding the pony."*

Eager young ensign Jack waits for his first ship assignment.

Jack's Navy and Marine Corps medal for his PT-109 heroism is pinned beside his Purple Heart in an outdoor ceremony at Chelsea Naval Hospital, Boston, in 1944, shortly before his back is operated on to repair wartime injuries.

my eyes, croaked a couple of times, but all to no avail. Out here, if you can breathe, you're one A, and "good for active duty anywhere" and by anywhere, they don't mean the El Morocco or the Bath and Tennis Club, they mean right where you are. See you soon, I hope.

Jack

Earlier, in the States, Jack was about to be assigned from Washington to the Panama Canal, which meant boring duty and no action. He got hold of Secretary of the Navy James Forrestal, a friend of his father, who got Jack transferred to combat duty in the Pacific. He was assigned to Rendova, south of New Georgia. And he was made skipper of *PT-109*.

On night patrol, August 2, 1943, *PT-109* was cut in half in the dark by a Japanese destroyer. Two men were killed. Jack was thrown on his back, injuring his spine again. Gallons of high-octane gasoline poured out and exploded into a sea of fire. The other PT boats presumed all hands were lost.

The front half of *PT-109* stayed afloat, however. Kennedy and four other men were on it. Five more were swimming in the fiery sea. Pat McMahon, the engineer, was badly burned and drifting away. Jack dove in and towed McMahon slowly back to the half-ship that was still afloat, saving his life.

The next day, the men had to abandon the ship's remains. They swam three miles to a small island that they hoped was not occupied by the Japanese. McMahon, wearing a life jacket, couldn't swim because of his burns. Jack put a strap from McMahon's jacket between his teeth and, doing the breaststroke, towed McMahon for five hours to the island, stopping every few minutes to rest and reassure the man.

When they all reached the island, Jack decided after resting to swim and drift all night in a passage off the other side of the island. He hoped to signal a boat with a heavy ship's lantern. He went out all night, but no ship came through. He swam back to the island in the morning light, exhausted.

On the third day the group moved to another island searching for food and water. This trip meant another three-hour swim, and Jack again pulled McMahon by his life-jacket strap. They found no fresh water except dew on leaves. The green coconuts and the milk made them ill. Their spirits were very low.

To get closer to the common ship lanes, Jack and Barney Ross swam to Nauru Island. They stumbled onto a Japanese shelter and found a keg of water, hardtack, biscuits, and candy. They also found a hidden one-man native dugout canoe. When it got dark, Jack paddled back to the others with the supplies. Next day he returned to Nauru to get Ross. A storm came up and the canoe was swamped. But, suddenly, a group of Solomon Island natives came by in a large canoe. They took Jack to Nauru and uncovered a second, two-man canoe. Using his jacknife Jack scratched a message on a coconut shell: "Native knows posit he can pilot 11 alive need small boat kennedy." He gave the coconut shell to the natives and indicated Rendova was the place to take it.

That night Jack and Ross went out in Ferguson Passage looking again for rescue by PT boats. They were swamped by a violent storm and almost drowned before getting back. In the morning they were awakened by four natives. One carried a letter from an Australian coastal watcher advising that rescue help was being arranged. It instructed Jack to come to New Georgia with the natives.

After taking a feast of C-rations to the other survivors, Jack lay flat in the canoe, covered with leaves to hide him from hostiles on the shore and any observation planes they might encounter. He was transported to New Georgia, where he directed a PT boat to pick up his crew.

In England, meanwhile, Kathleen and Billy wanted to marry. Religious differences, however, were not the only problem. Billy's parents and ancestors had been the ruling class in Ireland. They held the Irish in suspicion and low regard, and had a tradition of oppression and standing against Home Rule.

If Kick wanted to stay within the sacraments of the Catholic Church, her children would have to be raised as Catholics. Billy would not agree to that. So finally they were married in a small civil ceremony, which was not recognized by the Catholic Church. The duke and duchess, Billy's parents, were present. So was Joe Jr., who gave the bride away. He had supported Kick through the trials and anguish when her church and parents objected. She was always grateful to Joe.

Joe Jr. had completed two tours of duty. He was offered leave in the United States. But he volunteered for a dangerous, secret mission code

Kathleen, holding a tiny bouquet, marries Billy Hartington in May 1944, at Chelsea Registry Office in London. Joe Jr. stands behind with Billy's parents.

named Anvil.

The German V-2 rockets launched from the Continent were destructive beyond all other aerial attacks against England. The Allies had no way of destroying the bases used to launch the rockets. It was obvious, however, that some kind of exceptionally high-powered explosive power could do the job. Finally, a plan was devised to fly a stripped-down B-24 bomber with 25,000 pounds of torpex, an explosive having twice the power of dynamite, over the target and send the plane crashing in to explode on the sites. Two pilots would take the plane off from England and set it on its course to France, bail out, and let it be guided to the target by remote control from an accompanying mother plane.

Joe volunteered to fly a mission. By this time six of the drones had crashed out of six tries. Two pilots had been killed and two others crippled. On the morning of August 12, 1944, Joe and Bud Willy, his co-pilot, took the plane off from Fersfield strip

Outfitted in goggles, helmet, parachute harness, inflatable life jacket, and khakis, the student pilot, Joe Jr., poses on the flight line in July of 1941, six months before Pearl Harbor.

Joe (left), his instructor, and fellow cadets stroll the flight line at Squantum Naval Air Station in Massachusetts, readying for takeoff instruction in their training planes.

Joe Jr., sprouting a rakish moustache and looking older than his twenty-nine years, poses on an English airfield eight months before the secret mission that took his life.

Joe, Rose, Pat, Teddy, Bobby in seaman's uniform, and Jean at the posthumous award ceremony of the Navy Cross for Joe Jr. in Washington, D. C., a year after his death. The presentation was made by Admiral Gygax of the First Naval District.

Bobby, being sworn in to the navy at age seventeen in 1943 while Dad watches. He hoped to become a pilot one day like his brother Joe.

on the coast. They circled over England, reached altitude, and turned the ship over to the remote control by the mother ship. They were in the air twenty-eight minutes, over an area known as Newdelight Wood, when the plane blew up in two explosions.

Two priests came to the Hyannis Port house and asked Rose if they could speak to Joe. It was Sunday morning, and Joe was asleep upstairs. All of the family (except Kick) was at home, including Jack, who was back from the Pacific.

When Joe came down they told Rose and Joe about Joe Jr.'s death. Joe in turn told the children.

For his father, the trauma of Joe Jr.'s death was one from which he never truly recovered. He could hardly speak of young Joe in later years, nor could he read a privately printed book of collected memories by his friends and family, titled *As We Remember Him.* Joe Sr. had shared his life with Joe Jr., and an integral part of him was gone. It was agreed by all that Joe Kennedy was never the same man again.

Kick returned quickly to America to be with the family. She intended to wait out the end of the war at home. Billy was fighting on the Continent in the drive to Berlin. Three weeks later, the family had another visit. Billy Hartington, Kick's husband, had been killed by a German sniper in Belgium. Kick went back to England and remained there to live as a Hartington.

By 1944, the navy had enough pilots. Bobby, still in training, was one too many in the backlog. He was transferred to ship's officer-training school at Bowdoin in Maine, and then to naval ROTC at Harvard.

Bored, and also afraid he would not get into the war before it was over, Bobby asked for a transfer. But it was too late. He spent the rest of the postwar service on board a brand new destroyer, the *Joe Kennedy Jr.*, named for his brother. Life on board ship was like sailoring in *Mister Roberts*. Chipping paint, swabbing decks, observing the empty sea, and watching the radar scan miles of empty and peaceful ocean.

Kick, living in England, liked her life. She bought a little house in London, but she also lived the castle life of the Hartingtons. One spring holiday, three years after the war, she was flying from Paris to the Riviera in a small private plane with some friends. The weather turned bad over the French Alps. The navigation equipment failed, and the plane hit a mountainside.

"We lost our beloved Kathleen on May 13, 1948," her mother wrote in her diary.

Kick was buried at Chatsworth, the Hartington family's ancestral estate in Devonshire. Billy's remains are buried in Belgium where he died leading his troops.

The ordeal of war had been costly. There were wounds to be bound up in the next years.

Five years after Joe's death in the war, his father, mother, and a youthful Archbishop Richard (later Cardinal) Cushing (left) unveil a portrait of Joe at the dedication of a children's hospital in Brighton, Massachusetts, built by Joe Sr. in his son's name.

Vacations

On May 27, 1944, the war was better than halfway to its end. It was two days before Jack's twenty-seventh birthday. He was transferred from Miami to Boston's Chelsea Naval Hospital for a back operation. The surgery was to repair a deteriorating disk in his lower back, aggravated by the PT-109 adventure.

The operation was performed in July at the New England Baptist Hospital. By Jack's account, it was not entirely successful. In those days, back surgery was a last resort; it often left the patient no better and sometimes in a worse condition. "I think the doc should have read one more book before picking up the saw," Jack wrote to a friend.

Before the operation, Jack was awarded the Navy and Marine corps Medal. The decoration was presented in a small ceremony by the hospital C.O., Captain Frederick Conklin. Jack looked thin and frail in his full dress uniform. He wore the medal

Jack, Bobby, and Teddy looking like classmates in a high school yearbook. In fact, Teddy, fifteen years younger than Jack, is large for his age. Jack, skinny as always, looks younger than he is. And Bobby, eight years older than Teddy, is the shortest Kennedy brother.

next to another decoration, the Purple Heart.

After surgery, there was nothing more to do but surrender to waiting for one's strength to return. It was vacation time at home.

The Kennedys had three houses. Or, rather, one home and two houses.

One house was in New York City. It was from here that the children went away to boarding school. It was not really a place where they were together. A second house in Palm Beach stood on two acres facing the ocean, on North Ocean Boulevard. That one was for warm southern Christmases and short winter vacations. A tile and stucco house, built for the famous Wanamaker family of Philadelphia in 1923 by Addison Misner, it is large but considered modest compared to others on Millionaire's row.

Home, their real home, was Hyannis Port, on Cape Cod in Massachusetts. Here Jack came to rest and vacation with his family and wartime buddies. This was the place that all the Kennedys thought of as home.

That house sits in our memory like the family itself. We remember it, too, from many happy and sad occasions.

Hyannis was a resort town in summer. The streets were filled with tourists. They came to enjoy

Bobby and Dad, who puts his coffee down to give Eunice an affectionate embrace. Each summer for years the family watched the sailboats racing by at this end of the house.

the white beaches and to sail the inner coastline. There were clambakes, quilting bees, summer theater, and strawberry festivals. Downtown Hyannis always has the touristy smell of charcoal burgers, fresh fish on the waterfront, hot streets, and the clop-clop of beach sandals.

The Kennedys never built a home. In the late 1920s, when they went to summer on Cape Cod, which was booming as a vacation spot, they rented a house called "the Malcom place" for several summers running.

In 1926 Joe Kennedy bought the "Malcom place" for $25,000. The house stands on a quiet road leading down to the beach. Of all the houses around, it is the closest to the water. Bigger than it appears, the white, three-gabled place is large and rambling, with wide porches overlooking a long sea view. It sits on a large, green bluff at the end of Scudder Avenue. Well-tended lawns that slope down to wild dune grass meet a stretch of beach that is lonely but comforting to walk. The ocean water is cold to swim in even in August.

In later years, Bobby and Jack purchased houses on Irving Avenue. The several houses became what is known as the Kennedy Compound.

The Compound would become a political base, besides a home. It would be filled with news wires,

TV sets, a battery of phones, and conferences. And it would be circled by special police, reporters, Secret Service, and thousands of curious tourists on water and land. Today, bright lights are turned on Jack's house when evening comes, and the day guard is replaced by the night man to prevent vandalism by souvenir hunters.

Joe had the house remodeled by L. Franke Paine (the original architect) into fifteen rooms and nine baths. It has early American furniture plus some from the eighteenth century, giving it a worn, lived-in feeling. Grandma Moses, Currier & Ives, and English prints by Morland decorate the walls. There is a big family dining room where most events in the family were reviewed at mealtime and new ones debated.

When the kids were young, they played on the big porch looking out at the sea. On rainy Saturdays, when the air was cold and damp, they went to the movies and had ice cream in town. They had a near surfeit of movies; Dad was in the business. He built the first "talkie" private theater in New England in their own basement, next to the playroom. Twenty-seven seats and a wide screen. They had a piano downstairs. Rose played by ear and everybody sang. Ireland, in verse and note, came to life.

Rose, the house manager, put clocks in everyone's room. None could be late to meals on pain of no dessert. Lunch was served promptly at 1:15 and dinner at 7:30. Favorites were clam chowder, roast beef, and ice cream. Drinking milk was obligatory. The house used up twenty quarts a day.

They rarely went to bed late and always got up early. There was a governess for the older offspring and a nurse for the younger. The older could ride their bikes off the boundaries, but they had to be home by dusk. And if they forgot, Rose, who was Mrs. Discipline, went out in the blue coupe and ran them down like a sheriff after rustlers; a short sheriff who could hardly see over the steering wheel of the coupe.

She would leave notes everywhere for the children and maids and neighbors. Written on little pieces of torn paper, she reminded the kids to bring in bikes, the maid to cook a meal, herself to go to the dressmaker's, Teddy to pick up his Mickey Mouse sweatshirt behind the sofa. When she needed an extra servant she'd drive sixty miles to Boston to hire one herself. At the agency she'd avoid frightening the new help by admitting at first only to five girls. The four boys were skipped until the two were well on their way down to Hyannis, and she'd slip it in. Once, she said nothing, being cautious and having the boys arrive at the meal one at a time, fed in small doses so to speak. She was always the first up and off to Mass. She loved the little clapboard church, St. Francis. She had season tickets to the Cape Playhouse, and she played golf every day, doing the back nine, her clubs on her shoulders, through fog and stiff breezes, small greens and marshes. There were visits by Grandpa Honey Fitz, who would bring his store of political tales for the kids. Rose's brothers and sisters also visited. And there were famous people, too.

Life on the Cape was warm, informal, vigorous, and highly competitive. Of course there were the famous touch football and sailing contests.

Everybody present was expected to play touch football. Sometimes the guests even survived the experience. It's touch football, reported a visitor, but it's murder. If you don't want to play, don't come. If you do come, play or you'll be fed in the kitchen and nobody will speak to you. Don't let the girls fool you. Even pregnant they can make you look silly. If Harvard played touch football, they'd be on the varsity. When on the field, never stand still. Run on every play and make a lot of noise. Don't appear to be having too much fun. They'll accuse you of not taking the game seriously enough. To become really popular you must show raw guts. To show raw guts fall on your face now and then. Smash into the house once in a while going after a pass. Laugh off a twisted ankle or a big hole in your best suit. But, remember, don't be too good.

Joe's sport was boating and riding horses in the early morning. He said he liked it because it helped him to think and clear his mind. By the time Jack was out of service in 1945, Joe Kennedy in his post-ambassadorial days was out of the public eye and into the real estate game. It was no loss. He made more big money in real estate than he ever did on the market.

Competition against outsiders came in the sailing. The Kennedys had boats when they could hardly see over the gunnels. Driven to win, they developed a reputation at the West Beach Club as determined, dark competitors and hard losers. The races were not only hotly contested but, win or

Bobby shoots the shooter shooting Bobby. "Tuck in your shirt, Bobby," calls his mother.

Left: You've got to be a football hero to get along with a beautiful girl. Two worshiping beauties, Eunice and Jean, vie on their knees for Touchdown Kennedy's charms.

The old flagpole shot on the back lawn. How long can you hold a pose anyway! Too late as everyone but Teddy breaks up. Jean and Bobby stand with Teddy, and Jack and Eunice are in front.

The summertime gang: Jack, Jean, Rose, Joe, Teddy, Pat in a Harvard sweater, Bobby, and left-end Eunice with the pigskin. Teddy is down in front. Dinner will be served promptly at 7:30 tonight. Clam chowder, roast beef, and ice cream—everybody's favorite. But be on time, Rose orders, or you'll lose your dessert.

The house at Hyannis Port sits on a large, green bluff at the end of Scudder Avenue, facing the sea. The interior was remodeled in 1926 by Joe into fifteen rooms and nine baths. Although it was among several houses they owned, the Hyannis Port house was always called home.

Teddy and Jack (raising the mainsail) make ready to enter a regatta on Nantucket Sound. The young Kennedys were notorious for their competitive spirit. They hated to lose, and loved winning.

Four daughters: Kick, a barefoot Pat, Jean, and Eunice on the porch where they used to play together as kids when rainy days kept them home.

The tree and decorations are up for the traditional Palm Beach Christmas. Joe, in bow tie, holds Rose, dressed in slacks. Eunice rests a sisterly hand on tall Eddy's shoulder (she always called him Eddy), who crouches so that his shorter brother Bobby can get into the picture. Jean cuddles up to Pat's shoulder.

In the evening after dinner, the family gathers for a couple of hours of reading in the living room before a trip downtown to catch a movie.

lose, the passions got hot. After the Edgartown Regatta in 1935, the boys put on a party at a hotel that got out of hand, and landed them the night in Edgartown's small jail.

Rose once admitted that a weekend with the Kennedys could be exhausting. "Pooping" is the word she applied for it. Rose had special dispensation. She did not have to go boating. Urged to try it just once, she went down to the pier with Joe and boarded a Kennedy powerboat. It left the docks but stopped at the breakwater so that she could walk back.

After his Boston back operation, Jack went home to Hyannis to rest and think. It was in this period that the priests came to the house to tell them Joe Jr. was dead. And Kathleen left to go to Billy's funeral. And Bobby was in the service. And Rosemary was in the home for the retarded in Wisconsin.

The future? What to do in life now that everything had changed? Jack considered journalism, teaching, and politics. He began by moving toward journalism, working on a book of collected memories about his brother.

The breathtaking vista of Hyannis Port stretches behind the crowded side porch of the Kennedy house. The men, standing and seated among the Kennedy sisters, brothers, and cousins, are visiting navy comrades—Red Fay, Lennie Thom, Jim Reed, Barney Ross, and Bernie Lyons—from Jack's PT-109 days.

The New Generation

The rise, long march, and arrival at the White House took the Kennedys the next fifteen years. In that time, everyone would change. As they grew older, they married and produced another generation. New families were attached: Skakel, Shriver, Bouvier, Lawford, Smith, and Bennett in that order.

Even as they spent time in their own homes and their own family pursuits, strong clan feelings and the pursuit of politics would bring them together. They were adults influenced by two generations of politicians before them. It was virtually inevitable that someone in the third generation of Kennedys would become involved in politics. Still, the entry was slow.

Jack was retired from the navy on March 16, 1945, for a physical disability. War's end was six months away. He took no retirement, disability, or pension pay, but he did hold on to his GI insurance,

A twenty-nine-year-old navy veteran, who wants to be the congressman from Boston's Eleventh District, files for a place on the Democratic ticket in 1946.

the only life insurance he ever held.

He spent three months in Arizona, still trying to rest his back after the operation. Then he became a journalist. He served as a special correspondent for the Hearst papers, at the first United Nations meeting in San Francisco; after that, he followed the British elections and visited with Kathleen in England. But journalism he found wasn't to his taste.

By chance, a perfect opening came to get into Boston politics. James M. Curley, the renowned, wily *Last Hurrah* politician, decided to leave Congress. It was too tame. Curley was elected to his old job, mayor of Boston. He gave up the mixed Eleventh District, which he'd won by beating a Unitarian he once described as a member of a "curious sect who seem to believe that Our Lord Jesus was a young man with whiskers who went around in His underwear." The famous Eleventh covered East Boston, Joe Sr.'s birthplace, and the North End, where Honey Fitz and Rose were born. It took in Harvard's Cambridge, where Jack had gone to school, and three Irish sections where the Kennedy name rode high. A special election was to be held among nine Democrats who wanted the nomination. Victory meant Congress; Republicans were few and far between in the Eleventh.

The skinny navy veteran with the famous name takes to the microphone during his very first political campaign. He asks the crowd of ladies for their vote in the 1946 Democratic congressional primary.

Jack was a carpetbagger; that was one disadvantage. He grew up in New York, not Boston. He took his grandfather's hotel, the Bellvue, as residence. For the rest of his life his voting address became 122 Bowdoin Street, an apartment across from the State House on top of Beacon Hill. (Years later, he and Jackie were interviewed here by Edward R. Murrow for a "Person to Person" show.)

Jack was not poised; his public manner was rather shy. And he was skinny, boyish, reserved, and unable to talk with ward heelers and political hangers-on in their own language. He did not know, as they say, how to wear a derby. He was also out of place in the tough tenement neighborhoods of East

Boston, Charlestown, North End, and East Cambridge. A visit to a slum saloon was hard going. But he persisted, and one day his father saw him by chance on the street asking for votes. The old man was astonished. "I never thought Jack had it in him," was his classic remark.

Jack went on and on. "He went into alleyways and climbed the stairs of tenement houses where politicians had never been seen before," said Dave Powers, who worked for Kennedy, starting from day one until the end. "He didn't realize how surprised and how impressed those poor people were to find him knocking on their doors. Nobody else had ever taken the trouble to come to them."

As the primary went on Jack became less apologetic, more at ease, excited about winning, drawn into the art and tricks of politics, the day-to-day stuff of gossip, strategic moves, speechwriting, crowds, the busy business of the hotel head-quarters. Many young World War II veterans came

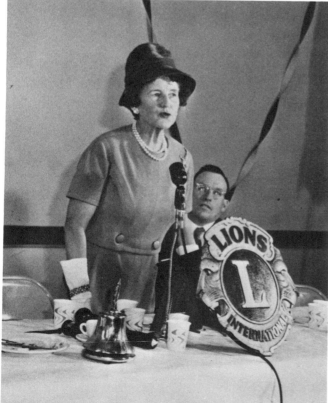

Campaigning vigorously on a Massachusetts street corner, Jack asks for the crowd's vote to send him to the Senate. The first time his amazed father saw the novice politican campaigning among a tough Boston street crowd, he remarked, "I never thought Jack had it in him."

Rose, a wise and long-time campaigner, takes on the Lions International crowd at a lunch in Boston on behalf of Jack's bid for the Senate.

Tough, seasoned political advice is given in the back of a limousine by the mayor of Boston, John Hynes, on the way to a fund-raising dinner to help Jack get reelected to the Senate.

Jack's Senate campaign brings the formidable Kennedy women to a famous tea party covered by early TV, that attracts crowds of women voters. Eunice shows off her JFK skirt. Pat (left) and Jean also wear them. Rose sticks to her conservative Paris fashions.

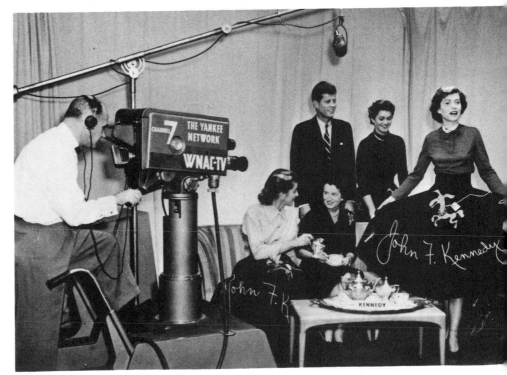

to work for him. He also brought in friends from his navy days. The ambassador supplied all the money he needed, and got some pros backstage to work for Jack.

His *PT-109* story as written by John Hersey came out in the *New Yorker*, so he ran as a war hero. "The New Generation Offers a Leader," proclaimed his campaign poster. On voting day his people hung around the polls wearing pieces of leftover army uniforms. And on the night of victory, Grandfather Honey Fitz got up and sang "Sweet Adeline." "That was the last real touch of traditional Boston Irish-American politics in the career of Jack Kennedy, the most phenomenally successful Irish-American politician of them all," *Time* magazine said later.

The style and pattern of politicking was set for his next three congressional campaigns, the two for the Senate, and the final one for the Presidency: using the young for hard, early organizing and detailed work and keeping control in the family.

There was one more decisive ploy that made a winner. "It was those damn teas," said defeated Senator Henry Cabot Lodge, who lost his Senate seat to Jack in a year when Lodge's man, Eisenhower, won big. He meant the campaigning Jack's sisters and mother put on, inviting women to vote for the son of a Gold Star mother.

Rose went into battle for her son's votes as if born to it, which she was. She toured the city, covering every religious, national, racial, and political cross section to be found. Leaving a posh dinner in a speeding car on the way to a union hall, she'd switch from a costly cocktail dress into a simple skirt and blouse.

Thousands of women received formal invitations on sleek white cards in hand-addressed vellum envelopes, announcing a reception for Mrs. Joseph P. Kennedy, and incidentally, her son Jack. A tea in a hotel. The women came to see the famous lady and listen. She put family touches to a speech no writer could compose. At the tea Jack gave a short speech after his mother had spoken. Then he invited the women to come up on the stage and meet Rose. The unbroken line sometimes went on for two hours. "Rose wowed them everywhere," recalled an old pol. "She greeted the Italians in Italian, and described how she grew up in the North End. In Dorchester she spoke about high school. At a high-society spot she'd talk about Jack, then she'd switch to Paris fashions. She wowed them."

Victory! The three-term congressman, confetti in his hair, arrives at his Boston campaign headquarters. He has won a Massachusetts Senate seat from Henry Cabot Lodge, Jr. by a good margin for 1952, a Republican year.

Life went on. The first of the young Kennedys to marry was Bobby, to Ethel Skakel. He met her when he was on shore leave from the *U.S.S. Kennedy*, at Manhattanville College. His sister Jean fixed him up with her roommate. "He was momentarily mad about me," said Ethel, "for two weeks. Then he took out my older sister, Pat, for two years. She was much prettier and more intellectual."

Ethel had a crush on Jack and helped in his campaign along with Eunice, Jean, and Pat. Ethel could have been born a Kennedy. Her family was wealthy, Catholic, and large. One of six children, she was at the bottom, like Bobby. She attended parochial schools and was an excellent athlete: swimmer, horsewoman, skier. She had the Kennedy energy and stamina. In fact, she was called more Kennedy than Kennedy when she became a wicked touch football star.

And so they had eleven children. The first was Kathleen Hartington, after Kick; a year later, Joe II; and then Bobby Jr. Looking over the large family, Rose once remarked, "I didn't know this was a contest."

Three years after Bobby married, Eunice wed Sargent Shriver. She met the ex-submarine officer at a cocktail party when he was working as a writer for *Newsweek*. The family called him Mr. Clean because of his sharp, forthright look. It took Sarge six years to sell Eunice on marriage. He ended up working for Joe in Chicago, where Eunice lived.

Five thousand spectators waited outside St. Patrick's Cathedral in New York, May 1953, for Joe Kennedy's daughter and her new husband to emerge. It was the first Nuptial Mass celebrated by New York's Cardinal Spellman in seven years. Seventeen hundred guests attended the reception on the Starlight Roof of the Waldorf Astoria. Eventually, Eunice and Sarge had five children, four boys and a girl.

Jack married Jacqueline Bouvier in September of the same year.

Pat married actor Peter Lawford. Four years earlier in 1949, she was working at NBC radio in Hollywood. Peter came in to do a broadcast. He invited her to a party at MGM, where he'd worked since he was a youngster. Born in London, Peter started in movies at the age of seven. He was now twenty-six, but he was not a Catholic. A later, second meeting came at the Republican National Convention, which Pat attended as an observer; Peter was a guest of Henry Ford II. They began to meet off and on. In 1954, when Peter agreed to convert to Catholicism, they decided to marry. But Peter had to pass muster with Joe first. That was an ordeal. At one time in history the church buried actors at night. In Joe's view, this was fine. "If there's anything I think I'd hate as a son-in-law it's an actor. And if there's anything I'd hate worse than an actor as a son-in-law it's an English actor," he said.

The meeting between Joe Kennedy and Peter Lawford took place in Palm Beach and was bizarre. Peter wore white trousers, a blue blazer, loafers, and bright red socks. As he described it, "Mr. Kennedy couldn't seem to take his eyes from the socks."

Mother Lawford, a Republican, evened it out. "I wasn't too happy about Peter marrying into the Kennedy family," she said during the presidential campaign. "Although I must say they've done well as a family."

The day of the wedding, a Sunday in June 1954, was a true Kennedy-Lawford event. Three thousand people were jammed outside the Church of St. Thomas More in New York. Traffic was stopped for blocks around. Jean was maid of honor. Jack, Bobby, and Teddy were ushers. They all waited for the famous groom's entrance at the baptismal font at the rear of the church. Suddenly, a roar from the crowd, and Peter the actor, had arrived. Afterward they all went to the Plaza for the reception, but not before being stuck in traffic, unable to move from the church, for five minutes. At the reception they greeted movie stars, royalty, and financiers—people like Barney Baruch, Greer Garson, and Prince Christian of Hanover.

Pat and Peter had three daughters, Victoria, Sydney and Robin, and one son, Christopher.

Jean was next. Two years after Pat's wedding, in 1956, she married Stephen Smith. They had dated when she was at Manhattanville College, and again when he was a second lieutenant in the air force and stationed at the Cape, and she was summering in Hyannis. Steve Smith was working in the family shipping business as well as doing time in the service, but he didn't like business much. He was a Kennedy type. He played ice hockey like a pro until he hurt his foot in the shipyard, and he was an excellent golfer and skier.

Good-looking and clean-cut, Steve was described as a "hard-boiled Freddie Bartholomew." He came from a political family; his grandfather had served three terms in Congress. "We may explain him," said Murray Kempton, "as another example of the tendency of sisters in large families to marry young men who remind them of their brothers. He comes naturally to the family style and family attitude." When somebody kidded Smith about marrying into a rich family he said simply, "My family had money before the Kennedys had money." Eventually, Joe took him into his business.

No Kennedy daughter ever entered into marriage in a hurry. After four years of courtship, Jean and Steve were married in the usual place, St. Pat's, by Cardinal Spellman. A bit of wind blew up Jean's veil of tulle and her orange blossom coronet as she walked up the steps from the limousine, holding a bouquet of white orchids and stephanotis. Eunice was matron of honor. Leaving a

Pat and Peter Lawford marry in 1954. Before the engagement, Peter underwent a stiff cross-examination by Joe Kennedy who believed all actors to be suspect.

The newly wedded couple toast each other with champagne during the celebrity-filled reception at the Plaza Hotel in New York.

reception at the Plaza's Crystal Room, bride and groom went honeymooning to Europe.

And they had two boys, Stephen and William. They adopted two girls, Amanda and Kym.

Last came Teddy, who married lovely Joan Bennett. Like Ethel, Joan met her Kennedy through a Kennedy, at Manhattanville College. She was typing an English thesis when her door opened. Her roommate told her to get over to the new gymnasium dedication or she'd be campused. The gym was a gift to the school from the Kennedy family.

Bobby and Ethel leave St. Mary's in Greenwich, Connecticut in June 1950. She, too, is from a large family, and is the youngest of six children. The couple met when Bobby was off-duty from the U.S.S. Kennedy and Ethel was sister Jean's roommate at Manhattan College.

Right: Teddy and his bride, Virginia Joan Bennett, emerge from St. Joseph's in Bronxville after their 1958 wedding. Jack, Teddy's best man, follows them.

Jean and Steven Smith, a New York shipping heir, leave St. Patrick's Cathedral after their marriage in 1956.

The Ambassador, who always loved dancing, takes a turn with Eunice
at her wedding. Teddy waits to cut in.

Eunice, standing on a shaky ladder, is
supported by her groom, Sargent Shriver, as
she takes an unsteady first cut out of the six-
tiered wedding cake baked for the 1,700
guests gathered at the Starlight Roof of the
Waldorf Astoria in 1953.

Eunice, the second Kennedy to marry, emerges from St.
Patrick's Cathedral on the arm of Sargent Shriver in May
1953.

At the dedication Joan sat near Jean Kennedy. They were friends. Jean said after Ted's speech, "I'd like you to meet my little brother." Little brother weighed 200 pounds and was 6 feet 2 inches tall. "He was my first and only love," said Joan.

Joan was a musician, modest and unassuming. Ted taught her to ski and to join in political doings. They were married three months after she graduated in 1958, again by Cardinal Spellman, at St. Pat's, recorded by a private movie crew. They went back to school to finish up Ted's law degree. He got it just as Jack began campaigning for the Presidency. Ted worked on the campaign full-time, so Joan had their first daughter, Kara, without her husband nearby. So had Rose before her, and so would Jackie after her. Two more children followed: Edward Moore, Jr., and Patrick Joseph, named after his grandfather. Joan and Ted did not have a home of their own until after Jack became President. And Joan learned that if she wanted to see her husband, the politician, she would have to join him in travel and see the world.

But it was another Kennedy wedding that was the national spectacle.

In the summer of 1929 Jack Kennedy was a stringy, tousle-haired twelve-year-old, enjoying the seaside beauty of Hyannis Port with his older brother, Joe, and his four sisters—Kick, Rosemary, Eunice, and three-year-old Pat. Bobby was toddling about the lawn in diapers. One hundred and twenty miles to the southeast, a dark-haired mother of twenty-one awoke one Sunday at Southhampton, Long Island, before it was light. She was unexpectedly hurried off to the hospital.

The doctor had promised Janet Bouvier she would deliver in New York City. Instead, the eight-pound girl was born at a small Hempstead hospital. The infant was a bit peaked-looking, it is said, and also more mature in appearance than most newborns. Christened Jacqueline Lee Bouvier, after her handsome father, Jack Bouvier, at the age of five months she appeared before the altar at the Church of St. Ignatius Loyola in a long-skirted christening robe with puffed sleeves and fine lace.

Thirty years later, on an extremely brisk and chilly January day, Jacqueline and Jack, now adults, walked arm in arm out across the White House threshold. On this day the lady wore a fur-trimmed coat and boots, a small pillbox hat, and a

Rose in a gown from Paris, her favorite fashion city, arrives at St. Patrick's Cathedral for the wedding of Eunice and Sargent.

fur muff to cover her white-gloved hands. He wore a dark topcoat over his formal morning coat and striped trousers. In his hand he carried a top hat. He wouldn't wear it. It felt uncomfortable to wear a hat. The two were on their way to his inauguration as thirty-fifth President of the United States.

Between the beginning years and this day a lifetime had passed. Ahead lay another so unique that only a handful of the millions who have lived in the United States have experienced it. For Jacqueline Kennedy, the country's new First Lady, even the slightest moment of privacy she had known would come to an end. She would be celebrated, imitated, pursued, and raised to the station of American princess. She would also find herself a criticized captive of her vast public.

No one comes prepared for the role of First Lady. There is not another life like it in the world to learn from. But the one so selected by chance can have inherent qualities of character that will serve her and help her cope in public life. Jackie had qualities that made her unique among First Ladies.

Jackie's growing-up years found her having all kinds of adventures. She got lost in Central Park in New York, learned to ride ponies, appeared in society columns on her birthday, wintered as a socialite's daughter in New York's fashionable East 70s, and summered in the Hamptons at the Bouvier home, Lasata, which is Indian for "place of peace."

Jacqueline came from old American stock. Her mother, Janet Lee, was affluent, well-born, and well-schooled. She spent her youth at Miss Chapin's and later studied at two women's colleges, Sweet Briar and Barnard. Her society debut was held at Sherry's when she was eighteen. Three short years later, on July 7, 1928, she married Jack Bouvier, who was sixteen years her senior, at St. Philomena's Church at East Hampton.

Jack Bouvier was a handsome man, sometimes called "the Sheik" or "Black Jack." Ancestors of his had come to America with Lafayette to fight in the Revolution, returning to France at war's close. One revolutionary son, Michael Bouvier, emigrated to America in the 1800s and prospered in Philadelphia.

Jack, his bride, and their five hundred guests enjoyed their wedding reception in the Lee House on Lily Pond Lane. The fashionable Meyer Davis provided the music. Afterward, the young couple were off on a cruise ship for a European honeymoon. Twelve years later, in 1940, they were divorced.

Janet Lee's daughter was obstinate, rebellious, but individual. This got her into hot water regularly and brought her to the office of the headmistress for a dressing-down. "I might not have kept Jacqueline—except that she was the most inquiring mind we've had in school in thirty years," said the headmistress of Miss Chapin's.

Next, at Miss Porter's school, bored at her turn as a table waitress, Jacqueline dropped a chocolate pie upside down in a teacher's lap. She was also the chief cookie snatcher from the locked-up icebox on Sunday evenings. She shared them with roommate Nancy Tuckerman, who was later to become her White House social secretary.

Jacqueline had a new father in thrice-married Hugh D. Auchincloss, a broker, ten years senior to her mother, whom Jackie called Uncle Hugh. The ex-Bouviers left New York and the Hamptons and went to live in winter at a Virginia estate, Merrywood, and in summer to Newport and Hammersmith Farm. Besides her sister, Lee, Jackie now had two new stepbrothers and a stepsister. In time, her mother gave birth to Jackie's half-sister and half-brother. Merrywood was a household of seven growing children.

By the time Jack was discharged from the navy, ran for Congress, succeeded, and spent three terms in the House of Representatives, it was 1952. Jackie was a grown woman. She had gone on to Vassar after Miss Porter's school. She had also been crowned Debutante of the Year by society's Igor Cassini, who described her as a "regal beauty . . . classic features . . . daintiness of Dresden with poise, soft spoken, intelligent, everything a leading debutante should be." In her junior year of college, Jackie went overseas and lived a year in Paris, in a ruggedly cold house with a poor and aged countess. After the Sorbonne, Vassar was uninteresting. So Jackie went to Washington, D.C.

Arthur Krock, the well-known *Times* columnist, helped get Jackie her first job. "I have a wonder for you," said Krock on the phone to Frank Waldrop, *Washington Times-Herald* editor. "She's round-eyed, clever, and wants to go into journalism. Will

Jackie at age five with a favorite puppy on the front lawn of her Long Island home.

An early love for horseback riding brings Jackie and her mother, Janet Lee Bouvier, to the exclusive Southampton Riding and Hunt Club with her father, John Vernou Bouvier III, in 1936.

you see her?"

Waldrop had thought for a long time that a woman, not a man, should do the "Inquiring Camera" column. It consisted of posing innocuous questions to some important Washington people, plus taking simple interview photographs. Waldrop told Krock to send his girl around and he'd see if she could do the work.

"Do you want to go into journalism, or do you want to hang around here until you get married?" Waldrop asked, with all the pithiness editors like to muster when testing a pretty female for a job.

"I want to make a career," said Jacqueline. What did he expect her to say?

"Well, if you're serious, I'll be serious," he said.

After telling her to be on the job and ready to go right after the holidays, he added, "Don't you come to me in six months and say you're engaged."

"No, sir!" said Jackie, understanding she'd been hired—at $42.50 a week.

In the end, Jackie didn't disappoint Waldrop. She stayed a year and a half before she quit to marry Jack.

Inquiring Camera girls are supposed to take pictures. Jackie got herself a quick course from the yellow pages on the venerable Speed Graphic, that large, boxlike foldout camera that has since departed newspaper work. She wasn't too adept, by her own admission. She would sometimes forget to remove the slide on shooting, thus no film was exposed. Eventually, however, she became an expert and also learned to write in good newspaper style. When she left, she received compliments from hard-bitten Waldrop. "Businesslike," he said. "Quiet, concerned, obviously very, very earnest in wanting to be a professional . . . self-sufficient, good at listening, and she handled her job efficiently."

Jack met Jackie while she was at work. She came up to interview him the same day she covered Richard Nixon. Their first meeting was a business visit and nothing came of it. The next time they met, Charles Bartlett, a writer and neighbor of Jack, invited the two to dinner.

Bartlett and his new wife had ambitions for these people. They liked them both and like most married people, tried to draw friends together, in the hope that something good would happen, as it had to themselves. Bartlett was on the right track.

At the end of the evening, Jackie and Jack walked out to her black Mercury, which was parked at the front of the house. Bartlett's terrier, Josie, hopped into the car when the door was opened, right onto a man sitting in the back seat. Who was the stranger? A clever beau of Jackie's; passing the house, he had recognized the car and had climbed into the back seat to surprise the lady. Surprise her indeed. There were obviously at this point one too many men. Congressman Kennedy froze, excused himself, and departed. No one recorded the conversation between the interloper and the car's owner.

Still, Kennedy wanted to court the lady. It began with an invitation to dancing one evening at the Blue Room of the Shoreham Hotel, a quaint suggestion for a man who danced poorly. Dancing in public ended that night by mutual agreement. In

A solemn Jackie, aged six, and baby sister Lee, two, on a 1935 vacation in Virginia.

Jackie, sister Lee, and a bored pup in an early Long Island photograph.

The newly engaged couple, ready for a warm-up game on the Kennedys' tennis court at Hyannis Port, will marry in three months.

Above: Jacqueline Bouvier, eighteen, was declared "Debutante of the Year" in 1947 by society columnist Cholly Knickerbocker.

Senator John Fitzgerald Kennedy, thirty-six, marries Jacqueline Lee Bouvier, twenty-four, at Hammersmith Farm in Newport, Rhode Island on September 12, 1953. The celebrated social event made national news.

The bridal party of twenty falls in for Jack and Jackie's wedding photo at Hammersmith Farm, Rhode Island on September 12, 1953. A wedding reception for eight hundred guests follows.

Jackie, for years an amateur painter, interests Jack in Sunday painting in the back garden of their Georgetown home.

subsequent weeks they dined with the Bartletts and played bridge, or they went to the movies with Bobby and Ethel.

Jack was getting ready to do battle with Henry Cabot Lodge for the latter's Senate seat. Touring Massachusetts for votes, he would call Washington from some oyster bar with a clanking of coins in the phone box and ask Jackie for a date between campaign talks. He promised to fly down on weekends to see her regularly.

The lady was no easier to win than the Senate seat. She went off to Europe to cover the coronation of Queen Elizabeth II for the *Times-Herald*. "Articles excellent, but miss you," Jack wrote after seeing her work. Like Pat Kennedy, who had gone on a world tour leaving Peter Lawford behind, Jackie let her beau live without her for a time.

The wedding was a public holiday. Thousands of people waited outside St. Mary's Church in Newport, Rhode Island. All the news media covered the wedding. (It had been postponed because *Life* magazine was coming out with an article about Jack as an eligible bachelor.) Hundreds were invited to the reception at Hammersmith Farm, where literally thousands of wedding presents were on display. The bride and groom, after a classic rice-throwing bon voyage, flew to Acapulco for their honeymoon.

What followed in their marriage has been

Ethel and Jackie watch a pair of star Washington quarterbacks warm up on a Georgetown ball field.

On a Sunday outing, Jack, Jackie (carrying the camera) and Ethel head for a ball field along a tree-lined Georgetown street.

Below: Bobby, Ethel, and Jack (in black sneakers) pose for Jackie, once a professional photographer on the Washington Post.

Look Magazine/Library of Congress

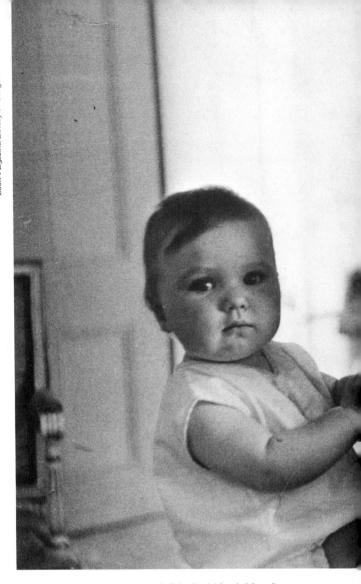

Baby Courtney, Bobby and Ethel's fifth child, adjusts her daddy's striped tie. Bobby's love and affection for all children was famous.

Caroline became the focus of curiosity and attention in the White House. Here she uses her fingers to go through a doll-counting session for mother.

Jackie, in a moment of quiet, sits on the second-floor stair landing at home.

John Jr. makes his first public appearance, wearing his father's forty-three-year-old baptismal gown, for his christening at the Georgetown University Hospital chapel in Washington. In two months he will move into the White House.

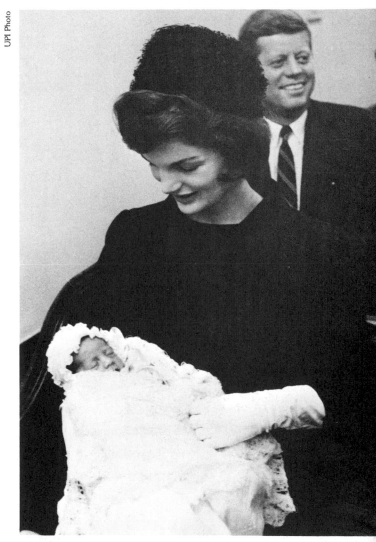

Kathleen and Joe Jr. give Daddy a hosing down in the backyard pool. Bobby was a famous horseplay artist with the kids—anytime.

Sitting on the front stoop of their Virginia home, Bob and Ethel show off the fruits of their six years of marriage. Kathleen, in front, is the oldest of the fifth generation of Kennedy-Fitzgeralds. The three boys are Joe (left), David, and Bobby Jr. Baby Mary is on Ethel's lap.

described as a difficult path. Jack's ambitions and duties carried him away from home much of the time. Jackie did not find herself at ease with, or drawn in any way to, politics. It drained her. The kind of compromise she realized was necessary, if she wanted to be with her husband, involved hotel meetings, crowds, dinners, and the like. It was difficult for her to stomach. But, to her credit, she gave of herself for seven years to something that was far harder for her to do than, say, for Ethel or Eunice or Rose, all of whom found politics stimulating.

What should have been happier first years for Jack and Jackie were spoiled because of Jack's illness. His spinal condition became progressively worse. By the summer of 1954 he was on crutches, which he openly resented. The best chance of regaining his health, doctors said, would be through a spinal fusion. But he also suffered from an adrenal insufficiency. He lacked natural defenses against shock and infection. On the Hyannis porch one day, Dr. Sarah Jordan of the Leahy Clinic said an operation offered a fifty-fifty chance of his recovering and risk of death.

Jack punched his crutches. "I'd rather die than spend the rest of my life on these things," he said.

That October he underwent a double fusion of spinal disks in Manhattan's Hospital for Special Surgery. Twice his family was summoned and Jack received the last rites. He fought back. After weeks of lying in a dark room, he was flown home to Palm Beach for Christmas. But his recovery was so slow that another operation was advised. In mid-February he returned to New York to undergo the second operation. Again he received the last rites, and again he survived. Late that month he returned to Palm Beach for the warm weather.

"He had a hole in his back big enough for me to put my fist in it up to the wrist," said Dave Powers. "He never said one word about what he went through at the hospital."

Jack was in constant pain. He was unable to sleep for more than an hour or two at a time. Jackie stayed with him day and night. He was in a room off the patio, beside the swimming pool. Jack would beg her to go out and enjoy the sun and water.

Then he got better. He began to write during the long hours. With the help of Ted Sorensen, his assistant, he worked on *Profiles in Courage*. It was published in 1956 by Harper & Brothers and became a best seller. The following year, it won the Pulitzer Prize.

UPI Photo

Jack, godfather to baby Victoria, holds the Lawfords' two-week-old infant during her christening at the Santa Monica Catholic Church.

When the spring of 1956 arrived, Jack was back in the Senate and back on his feet. It was in that same year that he made an important decision, the kind that changes a man's life. He went for the vice-presidential nomination at the Democratic National Convention in Chicago and was narrowly defeated. If he had gotten the nomination, it might have permanently foreclosed his political career as a national candidate, for Adlai Stevenson, with whom he would have run, lost to Dwight Eisenhower for a second time. Jack would have taken much of the blame, based on his religion.

About this time Jackie lost their first child through a miscarriage. She came close to death. Jack was not in America when it happened. He was in the south of France with his father, who was commiserating with his son over his defeat at the convention. Jack was not the first Kennedy, nor

Jack, working on a new bill in his Senate office, is here wearing his rarely seen glasses. They resemble his father's round, half-dollar style.

Jack, a member of the Senate committee on labor racketeering, confers during a hearing with Bobby, who is an acting legislative assistant on the committee.

The brothers Kennedy wearing soup and fish on their way into a press-restricted Gridiron Club dinner. The President usually attends and receives a political roasting.

At the 1956 Democratic convention in Chicago, Jack provided the narration for a keynote film in support of Adlai Stevenson. As he steps to the speaker's platform, he waves to a demonstration supporting him for the vice-presidential candidacy. He lost by a close count to Estes Kefauver. On the platform with him is Chairman Paul Butler.

1956
DEMOCRATIC

Jackie emerges from a Boston hospital wearing a cast on the ankle she injured while playing touch football. The cast was there for six weeks. She declared an end forever to her days as a touch-football player on the Kennedy All Stars.

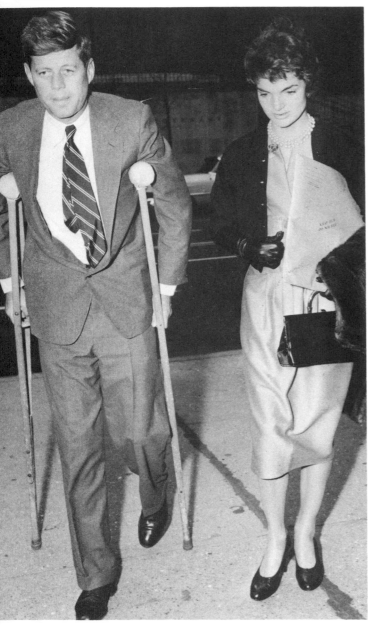

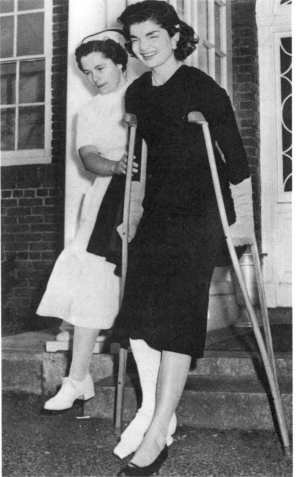

Right: *On the beach that fronts the Palm Beach home, Bobby and Jack stroll with Ethel and Jackie. They had come down to Florida to lay plans for the Presidential primary campaign.*

Joe and Jackie enter the Hospital for Special Surgery in New York. They have come for Jack's second back operation, a spinal fusion. The dangerous surgery brought him near death twice.

Rose sits proudly in the front row at the 1960 Democratic Convention with her son. The night before, the Democrats had chosen Jack as their Presidential candidate.

The damp swimmer is recognized and pursued by the female crowd on a Santa Monica beach. On impulse, he had left the quiet seclusion of the Lawford's beach house for a swim during a break at the Los Angeles Democratic convention.

Mrs. Franklin D. Roosevelt stops by Jack's table at a fund-raising dinner in Los Angeles, three days before the voting at the convention. She first supported Adlai Stevenson, and later switched to Jack during the campaign.

A hundred thousand New Yorkers turn out for a traditional ticker tape welcome for the campaigner. Jack and Jackie, wearing a pill-box style hat that soon caught on nationally, ride high on the back of a convertible down 42nd Street.

UPI Photo

the last, to be away on political business when his wife underwent a crisis.

In late 1956, because of his exposure on TV at the Democratic convention, and his winning the Pulitzer, Jack's stock ran high. He was in demand. He received invitations to speak all over the country. More than ever, he was convinced he could become President.

The road to the White House, through the primaries, the convention, and the national campaign against Richard Nixon, was long, circuitous, and filled with possible disaster. Jack organized a hard-driving political team. The decision was then made to get the nomination by proving in the primaries that he could win votes.

He first beat his front-runner competition, Senator Hubert H. Humphrey, in Wisconsin, which was Humphrey territory. Then he beat

UPI Photo

Jack returns to Hyannis Port for a week's post-convention rest and some sailing with Jackie. Soon he was on a grueling five-month national campaign for the Presidency against Republican Richard Nixon.

Campaigning in Los Angeles a week before election day, Jack's moving car fills up with confetti. Later he changed to an empty one to finish the parade.

Above left: *The largest street crowd of his campaign for President turns out along Seventh Avenue in the New York City garment district. Jack calls for a New Frontier in America.*

Humphrey again in West Virginia, ending forever the underlying issue of whether Jack could carry a state antagonistic to Catholicism. He could and he did. He went next to the Los Angeles convention and won the nomination easily. He then set out to beat the Republican, Richard Nixon.

Nixon claimed that Kennedy lacked the kind of mature experience in government a former vice-president would have. But in the crucial TV debates, Nixon seemed the inexperienced one and Kennedy the mature one.

The morning after the election victory, the adults in the family came into the Hyannis living room to pose for the now classic photograph of the Kennedys. The national win was small, only one half of one percent of the largest vote ever turned out in American history; but it would do.

The family gathering was breaking up; it was the moment of parting. The Secret Service was outside, waiting to escort Jack and Jackie to his public acceptance speech before the TV cameras set up in the Hyannis armory.

"Jack doesn't belong any more to just a family," said Joe. "He belongs to the country. That's probably the saddest thing about all this. The family can be there, but there is not much they can do for the President of the United States."

The new President and his family at Hyannis Port following election eve. This is the only picture ever taken of all the adults together. Standing: Ethel, Steve, Jean, Jack, Bobby, Pat, Joan, and Peter. Seated: Eunice, Rose, Joe, Jackie, Teddy, and Sargent.

While in her eighth month of carrying John, Jackie listens to Jack publicly thank her on television and radio for her campaign help, the morning after his election as President.

Right: Caroline walks her stroller and baby doll along a Georgetown street with a close friend. She moved into the White House two months later with a real baby in the family.

Camelot

The Kennedy White House, later called Camelot out of sentimental affection, lasted two years and ten months.

The inauguration took place on a Friday, January 20, 1961. Thousands converged on the snowbound city of Washington like a triumphant army. A raging blizzard covered the city. But the snow stopped by noon, and sunlight glistened over the icy white city. People stood in front of the capitol bundled against the cold. They were filled with lively excitement as they waited for the young President to take the oath of office.

Earlier that morning Rose had walked through the snow to Holy Trinity Church in Georgetown where a special Mass was being held, to ask God's blessing on the inauguration. A party had been held the night before, hosted by the Kennedys at Paul Young's restaurant. It had lasted into the early hours of the morning, almost to church time, but Jack had left early in order to study his speech at home.

Jackie and Jack depart for Versailles. Jackie, as a tribute to the French, wears a Parisian hairdo and a white silk ball gown by Givenchy. "Her appearance on this occasion outshone the multiple splendors of the Palace of Versailles," wrote an American reporter.

He came to the church later. He sat alone in an end seat, then knelt for the Preface and Consecration. Newsmen and the Secret Service stood by on the side and in the back of the church, watching.

Later that morning at eleven o'clock, Jack, still President-elect, and Jackie arrived at the north portico of the White House and were greeted by the outgoing President Eisenhower.

When Eisenhower came to office eight years before, he and Truman, the outgoing President, were on poor terms. Ike was still smarting from campaign remarks by HST. He did not visit with Truman. But now he asked the Kennedys in for coffee. They talked for a couple of hours about the house and servants.

Jackie, still recuperating from a cesarean delivery only eight weeks before of her son John, appeared to be healthy and tanned from resting in the sun at Palm Beach. But she wasn't really up to the inaugural day. They had been packing their Georgetown house belongings to move into the White House.

Just before one o'clock, the inaugural stand was filled. Rose, wearing dark glasses and a mink coat, and a smiling Joe, in top hat and frock coat, were seated in the southeast corner. Bobby, Teddy,

Eunice, Jean, and Pat sat farther back. Jackie, who attracted a healthy piece of attention away from the President, chatted with President Eisenhower on her left and Lady Bird Johnson on her right. She also stopped to speak with Mrs. Nixon.

"Now that was nice," said a girl to a reporter.

A radio writer covering the event for an out-of-town station said, "Everyone has to have a real hero just once. Kennedy's mine, and I think his wife is the greatest thing we've had in Washington for years."

After the swearing-in, Jack gave his inaugural address: "Let the word go forth that from this time and place, to friend and foe alike, that the torch has been passed to a new generation of Americans."

That evening, when the couple made their appearance at the Armory for the inaugural ball, the show stopped. The crowd surged forward to cheer the President and to stare at the First Lady when they took their seats in a front-row box. That kind of celebrity attraction would come again and again to Jackie—in Ottawa, Paris, Vienna, London, Mexico City, and other points around the world.

What followed in the next three short years would change the family's and the nation's destiny.

The first family change was Jack's decision to make Bobby his attorney general. Jack needed someone near him whom he could trust completely. Bobby could serve only if he had Cabinet authority. Critics said Bobby was too young and inexperienced. The President answered by saying he saw no reason not to give Bobby a "little experience before he goes out to practice law." To his credit, Bobby did well not only in the Cuban missile crisis, but also in his work on civil rights. And he was forthright in attacking juvenile delinquency, organized crime, price fixing, and many other evils.

Teddy, meanwhile, in a heavy-handed piece of political nepotism by his dad and his two brothers, got himself the Massachusetts Senate candidacy. Verve, excitement, superb showmanship—plus wealth, fame, power, and arm twisting emanating from the White House—did it. Teddy won in a runaway, 70 percent victory, although he barely made the age requirement of thirty.

Jackie was dismayed on moving into the White House to find so little of the nation's art and history reflected there. She started restoration work. Two hundred and forty pieces of valuable furniture and art were donated outright by Americans to the White House. Her restoration was stunning and was praised universally. The *New York Times* called it "family attic rummaging, one of the rarer American delights." Letters praising the First Lady poured in at the rate of about five thousand per week.

She was also criticized. Americans did not like her clothes, her reserve, or her treatment of her children. Or they questioned her wearing a wig, appearing on magazine covers, or buying from French dressmakers.

These were also great American days of pageantry, of prejudice for the arts. The essential character of the White House changed. Indeed, it set a path for the nation to follow. A French chef was hired. Gone were the potted plants. Lawrence Welk was replaced by Pablo Casals, Metropolitan Opera stars, Shakespearean actors, and Nobel Prize winners. Outside there were visits to the National Gallery of Arts, the Washington Ballet, the Old Vic, and the National Symphony. Jackie became our First Hostess.

Then came the first unhappy hint of trouble.

Joe Kennedy was playing a short round of golf at the Palm Beach Golf Club in December 1961. He was in Florida for the family's traditionally festive Christmas. He had spent Thanksgiving in Hyannis a week earlier with thirty-three Kennedys, mostly children. The bear of Wall Street was becoming a doting grandfather.

"I really don't feel too well today. It must be the cold I've had," he said as he teed off. He walked as usual, glad of the exercise. On the sixteenth fairway he had to sit down on the grass. Friends took him in an electric cart to his car. When he got home he told Jackie not to call the doctor. But she ignored his orders. He'd already had warnings of a stroke. He was supposed to take a blood thinner, but he wouldn't.

The doctor came, examined him, and sent him to the hospital. He had suffered an intercranial thrombosis, a blood clot in an artery of the brain, and it was inoperable. His right side was paralyzed and he was unable to speak. Over the next several years he alternately improved and deteriorated.

In August 1963 Jackie gave birth to Patrick Bouvier Kennedy five weeks prematurely at the Otis air base hospital. At first, all seemed well. But the baby developed a breathing difficulty. Though

Going without his coat in spite of the very, very cold temperature, Jack Kennedy stands to be sworn in as President by Chief Justice Earl Warren. Three other presidents of the past and future—Eisenhower, Johnson, and Nixon—also stand in the front row.

not regarded as serious, the decision was made to move Patrick by ambulance to the better-equipped Children's Medical Center in Boston. There he developed an affliction of the lungs that is common to premature infants. Oxygen could not reach the bloodstream. He was moved again, this time to Harvard School of Public Health. And there he died after two days of life.

"He was a beautiful baby," said the President quietly. He went upstairs to the hospital room where he had been sleeping and sat down on the bed and wept. Then he went to tell Jackie at the Otis hospital. At the private funeral, the President placed inside the small white casket a gold St. Christopher Medal that Jackie had given him on their wedding day ten years ago.

As his administration went on, the nation felt that progress was being made. The administration, called the New Frontier, worked on South American poverty, European military problems, peace, armament, the United Nations, prices, the Peace Corps, unemployment, civil rights, and much, much more.

The next year, 1964, was an election year. For most of 1963, Jacqueline was not expected to participate in politics to any extent. It was thought that Kennedy's voting strength was so great that no one could defeat him. Therefore, whatever support Jackie could give would not be needed. And since politicking drained her, it was unlikely that she would travel the hard and emotionally tiring campaign route that President Kennedy would have to follow in an election year.

But in November an announcement appeared on Jackie's behalf in the papers:

Mrs. John F. Kennedy feels she is needed and is eager to get into the political campaign swing in support of another Presidential term for her husband. Pamela Turnure said the First Lady wants to do as much campaigning as she can for her husband in 1964, limited only by her children's needs and her own health. While President Kennedy has not yet officially announced he is running for re-election his trip to Texas this week is

Eisenhower and Kennedy emerge from the White House after a morning's visit, to begin the traditional ride together down Pennsylvania Avenue for the inaugural ceremonies.

Right: America's President of a few hours walks down the snowy White House path with the First Lady to mount the reviewing stand for the impressive, four-hour inaugural parade.

Jack and his father in toppers watch a replica of the PT-109 torpedo boat pass in review at the inaugural parade.

Prince Rainier and Princess Grace of Monaco (the former movie star Grace Kelly) come for a White House lunch. The Princess's expression reveals an admiration many women felt for the President.

President Charles de Gaulle greets Jacqueline Kennedy and the President as they arrive for a state dinner at the Elysee Palace. Jackie and President de Gaulle conversed in French all evening. Asked to explain what he was doing in France, the overlooked Commander in Chief of the United States replied, "I am the man who accompanied Jackie Kennedy to Paris. . . ."

Stepping out to their first dinner invitation eight days after the inauguration, Jack and Jackie visit the home of a former Senate rival, Sherman Cooper, Republican from Kentucky.

UPI Photo

A moment's intimacy caught by the camera—Jack adjusts a wisp of his wife's wind-blown hair, while they wait in the limousine outside Blair House.

described as "political" and Mrs. Kennedy will go along.

Mrs. Kennedy has discussed her trip with Mrs. Johnson. Mrs. Johnson said, "All Texas is very excited about Mrs. Kennedy's visit, and they have laid out the welcome mat from Dallas to the LBJ ranch."

Thus, on November 21, the morning they were to take off for Texas from the White House for their first campaign swing together, President Kennedy waited in the second-floor executive office while Jackie was upstairs dressing for the trip. He was discussing some plans with two American ambassadors to African countries. John-John and Caroline were also upstairs, getting on their coats. They were going in the helicopter, too, but only as far as Andrews Air Force Base eighteen miles away. There they would all say good-bye, and Jack and Jackie would take off in the blue and silver four-engine jet, *Air Force One*. Their itinerary would include San Antonio, Houston, Fort Worth, and then Dallas.

As the helicopters landed on the White House lawn, the President, despite the slight drizzle, went out without a coat. Along came Jackie and the children with Maude Shaw, their nurse. They all climbed into the first helicopter; the second trailed along as security.

At the Andrews air base everyone got out and Jackie kissed the children good-bye. The children hugged their daddy. They watched as the jet plane lifted smoothly off the ground with their parents and a number of congressmen from Texas. As soon as it was airborne, other aircraft, holding special equipment for the President's trip, including the White House limousine, took off.

When the plane reached San Antonio the shouting crowds at the airport reached out through the lines to shake hands with both Jack and Jackie. The same thing happened at Houston, later in the day. The cheers were for both the President and the First Lady, and the President and his staff realized that the First Lady had a truly great drawing appeal despite the criticism she had received while living in the White House the past three years.

Jackie was bright and alive, surprising those who accompanied her with her eagerness to participate in the campaigning. She moved right into the crowds to shake outstretched hands. Reporters said she seemed to be having as much fun as her husband.

The President and Jackie surprised a meeting at the old Rice Hotel in Houston of a group called the League of United Latin-American Citizens. Jack spoke, and then said, "In order that my words may be even clearer, I am going to ask my wife to say a few words to you also."

Jackie rose and said, "*Estoy muy contenta de estar en el gran estado de Texas.*" ("I'm very happy to be in the great state of Texas.")

The crowd ate it up. When she finished, Jack walked over to her and whispered something. The Mexican band yipped with delight. There were cries of "*Ole!*"

In Houston, 200,000 people saw them. In San Antonio, more than 100,000 turned out. Again reporters were surprised by their complete and obvious enthusiasm. They concluded that the President would not do badly after all in Texas, where his star had not seemed very lustrous in recent months. "It's going to be one hell of an election, come '63," one reporter remarked.

The Kennedys spent the day at San Antonio and Houston, then flew on in the evening to Fort Worth, landing at eleven o'clock on a dark and rainy night at Carswell Air Force Base. To everyone's delight, thousands of people were here also, waiting to greet them. A crowd of perhaps 6000 stood outside a fence, blocking the entrance to the runways. They cheered again as Jack and Jackie, along with Texas Governor John Connally and his wife, were being greeted by members of the Forth Worth Chamber of Commerce.

To the anguish of the Secret Service detail, the President waded into a large crowd and shook hands, a big smile on his face. Both Jack and Jackie walked along the wire fences as hundreds of hands reached out to them. "Oh," said a teen-aged girl, "I'll never wash my hand again."

They rolled on in a motorcade from the airport, along Roaring Spring Road to the approaching night lights of Fort Worth, and arrived in the very heart of the city at Eighth and Main. Before them on the marquee of the Hotel Texas was a sign that said, "Welcome to Fort Worth Where The West Begins." A suite in the fourteen-story hotel had been made ready and inspected by the Secret Service.

The President's room cost $75 a day, which was $25 less than Vice-President Johnson's. The Kennedy suite, it was explained, had but one door to enter and exit, two less than the Johnsons' suite. The Secret Service preferred a suite with as few doors as possible to watch. The suite consisted of three bedrooms and a living room. A special telephone line linked up to a switchboard nearby had been installed by the Signal Corps. The suite was on the eighth floor overlooking a huge parking lot, where next day Jack would speak to some 4000 persons. Then he would go to a breakfast meeting for another 2000 people in the ballroom on the twenty-second floor of the hotel. Then the entire presidential party would fly to Dallas and Love Field, where Kennedy would ride in a motorcade at noon through the city to a special luncheon given by the Chamber of Commerce at the Trade Mart Building.

The next morning, their last, Jack went out to the parking lot, striding through the rain with someone holding an umbrella over his head that he seemed to ignore. He made his speech on a small foot-high platform. People were standing everywhere, even on the tops and hoods of their cars. All traffic came to a standstill. If there was any disappointment in the excitement of the early morning, just before nine o'clock, it was because Jackie hadn't made the meeting. Jack excused her tardiness: "Mrs. Kennedy is still organizing herself—it takes her longer, but then she looks better than we do." It brought cheers and laughter.

After the speech, he returned to the hotel and had breakfast in the ballroom. It was here that Jackie, who arrived late, made an entrance that caused the women to stand up on their chairs unashamedly to get a better look.

"And here's the one that everybody has been waiting for, here's Jackie Kennedy!" said the emcee. She wore a plum-pink rough-textured wool suit with blue pumps and pillbox hat.

A crowd of about 100,000 people watched in the streets as Jack and Jackie rode back again to the Fort Worth airport to fly the eight-minute trip to Dallas. No sooner was *Air Force One* off the ground than it seemed to be circling for a landing at Love Field in Dallas.

Looking out the window, Jackie could see the Texas skyscrapers and the prairie areas beyond the city. The President was working on the finishing touches of his speech.

By disposing of the "potted plants" and reviving the best in American furnishings and art, Jackie restored the White House. During the television tour she conducted for the American public, she leads us to the state dining room where haute cuisine was the new style.

A gathering of Nobel Prize winners, part of the White House cultural renaissance, brings novelist Pearl Buck and poet Robert Frost together with Jackie and the President for an evening of music.

Jackie converses in Spanish with her fellow guests at a luncheon in Mexico City given by Lopez Mateos, President of Mexico. Jack envied but also took pride in his wife's talent for languages.

The plane landed, taxied along the runway, and once again they could see a large crowd, perhaps 5000 well-wishers, in the warm sunshine. Those in the crowd cheered, waved welcome signs, and held flowers for the President and his wife. As the Kennedys came down the steps, someone handed Jackie a bouquet of red roses.

A delegation of political personalities was waiting. Again the President and Jackie reached out to shake hands and greet people, while the royal blue Lincoln pulled up to form the motorcade. Jackie was ready to climb in, but Jack was still shaking hands. "There he goes again," she said smiling, waiting for him to come along.

The Secret Service did not pull the plastic bubble-top on the car because it was far too nice a day, and no rain was falling in Dallas. The President's car with its familiar license plate GG-300 from the District of Columbia pulled up first in line. Jackie climbed in and took her seat on the left. Then came Nellie Connally, who took the jump seat folded down directly in front of Jackie. Next, Jack climbed in and sat in the back beside Jackie. Governor Connally sat down beside his wife on the other jump seat, in front of Jack.

Behind was the number-two car with the Secret Service agents. Third in line was the vice-president's car from the White House, with Vice-President Johnson, Lady Bird, and Senator Yarborough of Texas. Following them came the press car.

The motorcade started off. Crowds lined the route all the way, sometimes standing ten and twelve deep. They passed through the residential area, leading to downtown Dallas. In some places there were unfriendly signs, reminiscent of the trouble Adlai Stevenson had experienced shortly before he came to speak in Dallas. A woman had even gone so far as to hit him with a sign. But protests were much in the background. One could say it was a warm welcome the President was receiving.

In fact, by the time they had passed through much of downtown Dallas and were on Houston Street, Mrs. Connally said quite correctly, "Mr. President, you can't say Dallas has not been nice to you."

As the car, going at a slow ten miles an hour, moved around a small jog in the street off Houston at Elm, Lee Harvey Oswald waited on the sixth floor of the Texas School Book Depository Building while his co-workers were outside watching for the President.

That morning he had taken out the Italian-made .30-caliber carbine bought from a Chicago mail-order house months before, and wrapped it in paper. Asked what was in the package when he rode to town from the roominghouse where he lived, he said there were curtain rods.

Upstairs on the sixth floor he had opened the window that looked down to the street where the car would pass less than a hundred yards away. He piled up some cardboard cartons on which to rest the gun. Behind him he had built a wall of boxes so that if anyone entered, he could not be seen immediately.

As the President's car made the jog in the road to head for an underpass and onto the main highway, the watcher on the sixth floor fired from behind the President. The shot was heard by everyone. It was too loud for a firecracker, and there was a sound of concussion, too.

The bullet hit the President in the back. He pitched sideways with a small "Oh," toward Jackie. Almost instantly another shot rang out. John Connally had turned in his seat, and at that moment a second shot, possibly meant for the President, entered Connally's back, passed through his chest and out.

Connally pitched forward onto the floor. "My God, they're going to kill us all," he said. A third shot, the fatal one, struck the President in the head.

"O my God!" cried Jackie. "They're killing my husband. Jack! Jack!"

For a few moments all was dazed confusion. Jackie, who was cradling the President, let go and began crawling onto the back of the car for help as agent Clinton J. Hill pushed her back into the car and threw himself on Jackie and the President. In the third car, Secret Service agent Youngblood threw himself over Vice-President Johnson.

A photographer saw the rifle pull back into the window. Police began chasing up the grassy incline toward the building. The Secret Service men whipped out machineguns. Spectators with children threw them to the ground and covered them with their bodies.

The death car pulled out. "Let's get going!" cried the driver. They raced at seventy miles an hour down the highway toward Parkland Hospital at Harry Himes Boulevard. Behind it raced the vice-president's car, the Secret Service car, and the

Rose, arriving at the Palm Beach airport from Boston, is greeted by Joe. "I loved him . . . with all my heart," she said years later as Joe lived his last moments.

Before leaving for Washington from Hyannis Port, Caroline says goodbye to her smiling grandpa, who has been confined to a wheelchair by a stroke.

The President-elect's foreign policy discussion at Palm Beach is interrupted by Caroline, who decides to hold her own press conference now that she can fit into her mother's shoes.

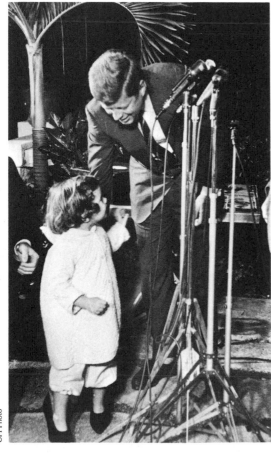

Spreading several major city newspapers on his table, Jack surveys the key stories. He had a reputation as a fast reader, and possessed an amazing ability for remembering a story's details.

Bobby was Jack's closest confidant in the White House. Jack trusted and relied on him whenever he needed an honest, bareknuckled answer.

The Founding Mother, who carries influence at the White House, gives her son advice at a formal Washington dinner. The President seems to accord it earnest consideration.

Jackie softly gazes out over the ocean as a breeze blows across the stern of the cruising Honey Fitz.

The summer of '62.

Left: *Enjoying an after-lunch cigar and the* New York Times *sports pages, the President takes in the sun and sea, which always restored his energy.*

Sitting under the boom, the President, always the navy lieutenant, can't resist correcting the Manitou's skipper. The family used the Coast Guard ship off Newport, Rhode Island, when they visited Jackie's parents.

Right: *Jackie on vacation in Italy in the August of 1962, waves to the photographers. Having slipped away from the Secret Servicemen to swim on a public beach, she drew a crowd and applause.*

A 1962 birthday photograph for Joe Kennedy. It is, in fact, a composite made up of four separate shots taken at Hyannis Port, Massachusetts and Malibu, California prepared by Cecil Stoughton, the White House photographer.

John F. Kennedy Library

Jackie, back to her old job as photographer (she once worked for the Washington Post), takes a snapshot of her husband and daughter on board the Presidential yacht, Honey Fitz, while cruising on Narragansett Bay.

UPI Photo

John Jr. receives a sweet, powerful hug from Dad while they play sailors in a weathered, beached rowboat on the Newport inlet.

A portrait of the Attorney General's energetic family taken in 1962. Standing, left to right: Robert, David, Michael, and Joe. In front are Kathleen, Kerry on Ethel's lap, and Mary Courtney on Bobby's. Four more children will follow.

Bobby, poking his head out of his office, calls for more coffee. His informal style was unique in the history of attorney generals.

A crisis in Mississippi over the enrollment of James Meredith, a black, at the state university extended to the Attorney General's office in Washington. Bobby confronts a host of reporters and explains how the federal government will attempt to solve the Mississippi civil rights problem.

Ethel gathers up the youngsters' coats as they leave the International Horse Show in Washington. The children sat with Bobby in the audience watching their mother on horseback take the jumps.

Ethel and Bobby enjoy a beautiful Colorado afternoon skiing the slopes of Aspen.

In June 1963, a special conference at the White House on civil rights brings the Reverend Martin Luther King Jr., (left), Bobby, Roy Wilkins of the NAACP, and Vice-President Johnson together.

Full of "vigah," John Jr. and his father leave Arlington Cemetery after ceremonies honoring those who fought and died to preserve this and every youngster's freedom.

Jackie, John Jr., and Caroline enjoy a late autumn afternoon of horseback-riding, one of their favorite sports.

The last thing Jack did before leaving the Cape was to kiss his father good-bye. The once vigorous, stately (now helpless) Founding Father was always taken out to the porch to watch his son depart in the presidential helicopter.

In the Oval Office two dancers show off a fancy Irish jig they've learned especially for the Commander in Chief of the United States. The Chief heartily applauds their talents.

Every kid needs a secret hideout where he can play or spy on people when he wants.

The nation's leader affectionately nudges his tardy son. John Jr., intrigued by the salute he received from the sergeant, delayed the takeoff of Air Force One.

press car. Agents called ahead on the radio telephone for special police escorts along the way.

Jackie held the President beside her as they raced down the highway. The panic had gone out of her.

The automobile came to a stop at Parkland five minutes after the first shot rang out. The agents ran inside to get stretchers. The President had not stirred; Connally was conscious, but numb and vaguely aware he was in pain and badly shot.

A reporter ran over and looked inside. The President was facedown in the back seat of the car. Jackie had him in her arms and was whispering something to him. Connally was on his back on the floor of the car, his head and shoulders cradled in the arms of his wife.

"How badly was he hit, Clint?" the reporter asked the chief of the Secret Service detail.

"He's dead," Hill replied.

Jackie, her skirt, stockings, and shoes covered with blood, the roses crushed on the floor under Connally, helped get the President out of the car and onto the stretcher. She kept her hand on his form as they walked into the hospital.

Police quickly surrounded the entrances. Senator Yarborough related what he could remember of the shooting to the newsmen who had pulled up behind him in their own car.

Inside, surgeons operating on Connally heard him say, "I think they shot me from the back. They shot the President, too. Take care of Nellie."

The President was unconscious. Drs. Malcolm Perry and Kemp Clark, chief neurosurgeon, examined the wound with the help of eight other doctors. They worked for forty minutes, giving him blood transfusions and oxygen. They performed a tracheotomy to help his breathing. They fed fluids into him and attached an electrocardiograph to record his heartbeat. There was no action. They tried closed-chest massage.

"It was apparent," said one doctor later, "that the President was not medically alive when he was brought in. There was no spontaneous respiration. He had dilated fixed pupils. Technically, by using vigorous resuscitation, intravenous tubes and all the usual supportive measures, we were able to raise a semblance of heartbeat. But, to no avail."

Caroline kisses her father's hand. She carries a bouquet of daisies to give her mother, who is resting at the Otis Air Base Hospital following the death of their infant son, Patrick Bouvier.

Jackie stood by in the operating room. She would not leave. A young medical student described her like an animal that had been trapped, "like a rabbit—brave, but fear was in the eyes."

At fifteen minutes before one o'clock, the Very Reverend Oscar L. Huber arrived in the emergency room. He drew back a sheet that covered Jack's face and anointed his forehead with oil. "I absolve you from all censures and sins in the name of the Father and of the Son and of the Holy Spirit, Amen. If you are living, may the Lord by this holy anointing forgive whatever you have sinned. Amen. I, by the faculty given to me by the Apostolic See, grant to you a plenary indulgence and remission of all sins and I bless you. In the name of the Father and of the Son and of the Holy Spirit. Amen."

Then he, Jackie, and others in the room prayed, covering the face once more. "Our Father, Who art in Heaven . . ." and "Hail, Mary, full of grace . . ."

The police of Dallas searched for the gunman, who had escaped in the crowd, later killing Officer J. D. Tippit with a revolver. Lee Harvey Oswald, soon captured in a downtown movie theater, was accused of both shootings.

President-to-be Lyndon Johnson, now surrounded by a contingent of Secret Service agents, was hurried to the airport to make ready to return to Washington. A white Cadillac hearse brought a bronze casket to the hospital. Jack's body was placed inside. Jackie took her wedding ring from her left hand and slipped it onto the President's finger. She now had in her possession Jack's new St. Christopher medal, the one she had given him to replace the medal they had buried with Patrick at the Brookline cemetery in Boston in August.

"Do you think it was right? Now I have nothing," said Jackie numbly to Kenny O'Donnell.

"You leave it where it is," he said.

The bronze casket, taken out of the hospital with Jackie beside it, was driven to the airport where they had landed three hours before.

A small, trim woman of sixty-seven, Federal Judge Sarah Hughes, had been called long-distance by the U. S. Attorney General's office in Washington and had been given the official oath of office for the new President to take. She would administer it to Johnson. She had ridden out to the Dallas airfield carrying her Bible and the written oath. Police stopped her, checked her story, then let her through. She boarded *Air Force One*, where Jackie, President Johnson and his wife, Lady Bird, plus aides of the dead President were waiting.

Placing his hand on the Bible, Johnson said, repeating after Judge Hughes, "I do solemnly swear that I will faithfully execute the office of the President of the United States, and will to the best of my ability, preserve, protect and defend the Constitution of the United States of America."

"So help me, God," added Judge Hughes. It was not in the oath, but she felt it should be added.

"So help me, God," said Lyndon Johnson, now the thirty-sixth President of the United States. John F. Kennedy had been dead little more than one hour and thirty minutes.

President Johnson embraced his wife, kissing her on the cheek. He turned to Jackie and embraced her. He put his arm around Evelyn Lincoln, JFK's secretary.

The White House physician suggested that Jackie take a sedative, or at least rest and not remain to watch over the casket. But she would not leave it.

Air Force One waited only until Judge Hughes disembarked. Then the plane took off from Love Field for the two-and-one-half-hour flight to Andrews Air Force Base.

Dave Powers, Brigadier General Godfrey McHugh, Larry O'Brien, and Kenny O'Donnell sat with Jackie beside the casket.

President Johnson called Rose Kennedy on the radiophone. She had been informed at Hyannis, as had Eunice and Ted in Washington, Bobby and Ethel in Washington, Peter Lawford in Las Vegas, Pat at Los Angeles, and the Steven Smiths in New York. The one person not told was Joe Kennedy, at least for the time being.

"I wish to God that there was something I could do. I just wanted you to know that," said the new President to Rose. He asked Lady Bird to speak. "We feel like the heart has been cut out of us. Our love and our prayers are with you," she said.

A call was then made to Nellie Connally to reassure her. Connally was in critical condition, but it appeared certain that he would live.

As the plane made its way back to Washington, Jackie asked that a message be sent to the Bethesda Hospital asking them to prepare to embalm the body for burial. Later the similarity of her husband's death to that of Abraham Lincoln, along with her knowledge of the history of the

White House, helped her to decide certain of the funeral arrangements. She had someone telephone artist William Walton to bring a book on Lincoln's death from the White House library that showed drawings and photographs of Lincoln lying in state.

The plane set down at Andrews Air Force Base in the late dusk. The terminal was blazing with floodlights. As the plane rolled to a stop, Bobby rushed up the ramp, went through the plane, and folded Jackie in his arms. She wept and asked him, "Would you come with us?"

Inside the plane, everyone waited while a yellow cargo car rolled out to the rear door. Larry O'Brien, Dave Powers, and Kenny O'Donnell lifted the casket onto the large lift and stepped on to ride it to the ground.

Pallbearers in uniform shifted the heavy casket onto a military ambulance. A black Cadillac was waiting for Jackie, but she would not use it. Instead, she went to the gray ambulance. She hadn't the strength to open the door. They did it for her. She climbed into the back, not the front, to ride with the body. Bobby was with her when they drove off through the white-gloved honor guard to the hospital.

At the hospital they had expected the body to arrive by helicopter and had posted an honor guard at the hospital's helicopter landing pad. A crowd of perhaps 3000 people had gathered outside the hospital in the dark for the arrival.

Jackie remained at the hospital. Several times she was offered sedation by Dr. John Walsh, along with the suggestion that she return to the White House for some sleep. She refused both.

Late that night, Kenny O'Donnell returned her marriage ring to her.

When the President's body was taken back to the White House in a wooden casket, Jackie went with it to the East Room in the Saturday morning dawn. She supervised the preparation of the catafalque and the dark drapes. "Couldn't the honor guard include a member of the Special Forces?" she asked, referring to the guerrilla-trained troops that Jack had a strong interest in. Thus one more soldier, in a green beret, was added to the honor guard.

Then Jackie went to find her two children. This week would be John-John's birthday. The day they would bury his father he would be three years old. Two days later, Caroline was to have her sixth birthday.

Welcome to Dallas. The
presidential jet has landed at
Love Field. Jackie holds a
bouquet of roses as she, Jack,
and Governor and Mrs. Connally
get into the limousine for the
eleven-mile motorcade.

The assassination—Dallas,
November 22, 1963, taken by a
spectator with a Polaroid camera.

The children had had their supper the night before with Grandma and Grandpa Auchincloss. They had been told of their father's death by their grandmother.

The scene between mother and children has not been recorded. But many people know the experience of having to explain to their child the death of a mother or father. The words are there, but the meaning is difficult to convey. It may seem confused to a six-year-old. To a three-year-old it seems one explanation for the parent's temporary absence.

On Saturday morning Jackie took the children down to the East Room to see the casket and to be part of the family Mass. The closed mahogany casket—never opened again—reflected the flickering candlelight. It was the first Roman Catholic Mass celebrated at the White House. The Reverend John Cavanagh, an old family friend, officiated. Present were perhaps seventy-five friends and relatives.

Ethel and Bobby, Jean and Stephen Smith, Pat and Peter Lawford, Sargent Shriver, and Joan Kennedy were at the White House. Eunice and Ted had gone to Hyannis to see Rose, who would come to the White House the next day.

They did not tell Joe the news that night. But he understood something was wrong. The next day he was in his room with Ted and Eunice and asked that Ted turn on the television, which, of course, had nothing on but the coverage of the assassination and its aftermath. Ted replied that the set was broken. Joe pointed to the disconnected cord. Ted plugged it in, turned on the set, then suddenly jerked the cord from the wall. Then he broke the news to Joe.

"He took it very well," said Ted the next day, without elaborating for the newsmen.

After the White House Mass, Jackie retired, and the procession of dignitaries, including former President Eisenhower, senators, governors, and foreign officials began arriving in the rain. Former President Truman visited the East Room, then asked for Jackie and visited with her upstairs for another fifteen minutes. The public did not see her again until the next morning. That day, the body of her husband would leave the White House and proceed to the Capitol rotunda for viewing by the public all day and night.

On Sunday afternoon President Johnson and Lady Bird left their home in Georgetown in a limousine and arrived at the White House just before one o'clock. Behind them came the empty caisson draped in black and drawn by six gray horses. This was the same caisson used to carry President Roosevelt's body from the White House to the Capitol in 1945. The honor guard, from the ceremonial "Old Guard" regiment at Fort Meyer, Virginia, rode three of the gray horses on the left side of the caisson.

Behind came a riderless, dark horse, named Blackjack after the famed General Pershing. The lone horse represented a tradition dating back to the days of Genghis Khan, when the soldier's mount was sacrificed in the belief that his spirit accompanied his master to heaven. Lincoln's funeral had his own horse, and his riding boots in the stirrups. Roosevelt's funeral had a riderless horse, wearing a hood and sheathed in black; the stirrups were inverted with a sword placed through them. Blackjack, a skittish sixteen-year-old led by Private First Class Arthur Carlson of Alabama, had a pair of polished black riding boots reversed in the stirrups. A sword in scabbard hung from the black saddle.

The eight-man guard that had been posted all night in the East Room lifted the heavy casket off the catafalque and carried it out the black-draped White House entrance, down the steps, and onto the caisson. They moved to the front. The President's military aides formed behind.

Jackie, the children in hand, wearing a black suit and black lace mantilla, came out of the house. Caroline in a blue coat wore a black ribbon in her hair. The caisson moved off a little and halted. The black limousine slid up to the foot of the steps. Young John-John hopped in and onto the seat to stare out the back window. Jackie and Caroline followed. Then came Bobby. President Johnson and Lady Bird took the two front jump seats. Other cars followed with Patricia, Jean, Peter, and Steven. In a third car were Jackie's mother and stepfather and other Auchincloss family members. Ethel and six of her children, with Sargent, came next. Rose, Teddy, and Eunice were still in Hyannis. Following came the White House staff, security agents, and police.

The two-block-long procession was slow, paced at a hundred steps a minute by the walk of those in front of the caisson. In the lead up Pennsylvania Avenue was the police escort commander, Major General Philip Wehle of the Military District of Washington, with five soldiers and muffled drums, a drum major beating slow time, and a company of navy enlisted men.

Behind them came the special honor guard composed of the Joint Chiefs of Staff and the President's military aides. Then the American flag, followed by the caisson, the single horse Blackjack, and the car with Jackie and the children.

At twenty-five-foot intervals along the route soldiers stood with bayonets at parade rest. Behind them crowds ten deep, and sometimes twice that, lined the streets, hung from building windows, and stood on the pedestals of the street's many statues.

Some cried, though for the most part they were dry-eyed and silent. It was a family crowd, dressed in Sunday clothing. Some children came forward and sat on the curb. Others were perched on the shoulders of their fathers.

One aged black woman with tears streaming down her cheeks said, "My God, I never thought I'd live to see this day."

As the caisson passed, the military details along the street snapped to attention and presented rifles in salute. Men removed their hats and some women pressed tissues to their eyes. The hawkers before the deserted government building stopped selling their twenty-five-cent postcards and the white-bordered pictures of the slain President that cost a dollar.

The silent crowd was almost unmoving along the first blocks as each element of the parade passed. But as newsmen and photographers permitted to follow at the end of the parade passed by, people from the curbs fell in behind the procession. Some moved ahead of the newsmen and attempted to walk beside the cars. The police formed a cordon across the avenue and stopped all civilians but the newsmen. But, after a few more blocks, the crowds again fell in; at last the marines formed with fixed bayonets across the street and stopped everyone, including the newspaper people.

The procession moved into the Capitol area, where 35,000 persons had gathered to wait and watch.

The caisson halted forty-five minutes after it had left the White House. A twenty-one-gun salute boomed out, echoing over the vast plaza. "Hail to the Chief" was played at slow beat.

The "Navy Hymn," at Jacqueline's request, began as the casket was borne up the long steps by the eight guards. The mourners followed the casket up the steps into the rotunda. Inside a red-velvet rope on gold stands made a circle perhaps twenty-five feet from the catafalque, the same that had held Lincoln's body. Congressmen, Cabinet members, and other dignitaries gathered.

The Kennedys were all together. Caroline became restless only once. Young John-John was taken after a while to the Capitol Office Building and given one of the small flags. He wanted to "take it to my daddy."

Senator Mike Mansfield eulogized the President. He spoke of his bravery and the life he had lived for his country. And then he spoke of Jackie: "In a moment, it was no more. And so she took a ring and placed it on his hand, and kissed him, and closed the lid of a coffin."

Jacqueline Kennedy stood with regal bearing, head up and silent. Bobby listened with tears rolling down his face. Then Jackie, with Caroline in hand, approached the coffin of her husband. "Kneel down," she said to Caroline softly. Together they knelt and Jackie kissed the coffin, while Caroline reached out to touch the flag. "Everyone . . . everyone was profoundly moved when they saw her do this," said one senator afterward. "It was a surprise, but it was the right thing. God, how touching it was."

Everyone filed out slowly to the bottom of the long steps. At the foot they stood talking in the afternoon light. Then Jackie and the children left with Bobby in the car. The body of the dead President lay in state for the public to view.

While thousands were lining up in the streets to pass through the rotunda, more people poured into the Capitol by car and rail and bus to pay their respects to the late President. Later that night, after nine o'clock, Jackie and Bobby returned unannounced. She walked into the rotunda on Bobby's arm. They halted at the rope that held the crowd. There was absolute silence; the room was still.

She walked slowly and knelt beside the coffin once again, her hand on the flag, and kissed the coffin. Then she rose with tears streaming down her face and walked outside and down the steps, looking into the faces of the crowd as she descended. At the bottom, she refused the car and murmured, "Let me walk, let me walk." A middle-aged woman, when she recognized the First Lady, broke into tears and embraced her. They spoke together. When the woman was asked what they had said, she replied, "Nothing . . . nothing," and walked away in tears.

Later, other Kennedys came to the rotunda. Rose, Peter, Pat, Ethel, and Joan went as a group

A tear falls on her veil as Jackie leaves the grave, holding the folded flag that draped the coffin. She gave the flag to his father to keep.

Robert takes Jackie's hand at the grave after three final salvos of rifle fire and the playing of "Taps." The funeral is over.

As the casket is carried down the cathedral steps and placed on the caisson to be drawn by the six white horses to the Arlington grave, a son gives his father a farewell salute.

The caisson carrying Jack Kennedy's body is followed by the riderless horse Black Jack, the family, and the world's leaders as they walk together in the funeral cortege to St. Matthew's Cathedral for the Mass.

*The family leaves the Capitol. The casket remained in the rotunda
all day Sunday, November 24, 1963. A pensive quiet hung over the
Capitol. People, who waited in lines that extended for blocks,
passed through the rotunda to pay their last respects.*

to the left-hand side of the catafalque. All except Peter knelt for a short time and then left. Later, Lee Radziwill entered the rotunda and knelt briefly, leaving by the side entrance with a Secret Service agent.

As Jackie and Bobby walked down the plaza along the west side of the building, they came upon a group of nuns in line, Sisters of Mercy. Mother Mary Regina, the head of the order, stepped forward and spoke to Jackie. At that point, the crowd suddenly recognized Jackie and Bobby; they got into a car and drove off.

As the night hours came on, people on line had to endure the cold. At eleven o'clock, one congressman who drove the length of the line reported it to be nine miles long. It had begun moving immediately after the ceremonies at three o'clock when Secretary of the Navy Paul Nitze and his family left. Mourners tramped across the cold stone floor two abreast, about sixty people a minute; by eleven o'clock, more than 50,000 had passed the bier. "He's my President and I've come to see him," one young man said simply.

People came in chartered buses from as far away as the Midwest. Many drove all night. Some who had started late decided to turn back when it was announced that people standing at the rear of the line would never reach the bier by ten in the morning, when the casket would be removed for the funeral cortege.

The guards doubled up the line to four abreast. "Please keep moving. Please keep moving. There are lots of people waiting outside," said one guard quietly.

It was a young crowd at first, young girls and young men—college students, soldiers, and teen-agers. They were wrapped in blankets to ward off the cold, and stomped their feet and chatted quietly. Many were in tears.

Later, the crowd grew older, with many middle-aged and elderly persons. Families with children in strollers, the blind with sighted persons, people with black armbands or black ties; they passed by the casket and cast their shadows briefly across the catafalque and the four enlisted men standing at the corners in absolute stillness.

They saw a simple wreath of red and white carnations with a red, white, and blue ribbon from President Johnson. Many, though they had been asked not to, surreptitiously took photographs. Many reflected the historic import of the night. One marine lieutenant colonel with four children was

asked why they held so long a vigil. "I felt the children would want to say in years to come that they had actually been here," he said.

In the late night, men in American Legion uniforms, Cub Scouts, a girl on crutches; they all inched along in the 40-degree cold. One spoke for all. "It isn't cold out here,'" he said quietly.

At eight o'clock the next morning, those who were more than two blocks away were told they could not enter; the police cut off the line. Late arrivals had been warned of this at hourly intervals beginning at 2:00 a.m. but people still came and waited. Estimates were that 140,000 persons had passed through. Among the last to do so was former Vice-President Richard Nixon. The massive doors to the Capitol were closed promptly at nine o'clock. Five minutes later, the last of the mourners passed out of the great hall.

On the morning of the third day, which dawned clear and brilliant, Jacqueline Kennedy emerged from the White House with Caroline and John-John. This day she was to bury Jack. It was also the official mourning day for the nation—stores, banks, theaters, schools, markets, and offices. Throughout the nation, people would stay by their television sets, as they already had for hours, to watch the funeral cortege go to St. Matthew's Roman Catholic Church, where Mass would be celebrated by Richard Cardinal Cushing. The cardinal, an old friend of the Kennedy family and especially close to Rose through the years, had married Jack and Jackie at Hammersmith Farms. He had christened their children. He had also buried Patrick four months before.

This was also the day Jackie was to rise to majesty. Already she had borne herself with regal firmness in public throughout the two days of ceremonies that left a watching nation awed by her strength. This day she would appear magnificent as she marched proudly behind her husband's casket, leading chancellors, presidents, kings, princes, ambassadors, senators, and generals through the street to the church.

She had arranged much of the funeral's protocol. She asked that Britain's Royal Highland Black Watch, which Jack had enjoyed from the White House balcony a week before, be invited. She asked Ireland's Irish Guards, which he had seen on his trip with Eunice, to come also. And she had requested the U.S. Air Force's ceremonial bagpipes to appear at Arlington and to wail off over the hill in an exit that had once thrilled her husband at the White House. "He really belongs to the country as a whole," she had said, and so she decided to bury him at Arlington rather than in the family plot at Brookline. She asked that Luigi Vena, who had sung at their wedding, sing the "Ave Maria" at the cathedral. And that *Air Force One* fly over in salute at the grave. And finally, she suggested that at Arlington an "eternal light" be placed at the head of the grave, to be a reminder of this day and of this man.

The nation's capital was filled with the largest gathering of heads of state ever seen in modern times. It included France's President Charles de Gaulle, Germany's Chancellor Ludwig Erhardt, England's Prince Philip and Prime Minister Douglas-Home, Russia's Deputy Premier Anastas Mikoyan, the United Nations' Secretary General U Thant, Belgium's King Boudouin, Greece's Queen Frederika, and Ethiopia's Emperor Haile Selassie. There were twenty-two prime ministers and presidents. Ruling monarchs, princesses, and princes came from nine countries; officials from another fifty countries, including Asia, Africa, the Middle East, South America, and Europe, took part. Two hundred and twenty persons, representing ninety-two nations, five international agencies, and the papacy, came to Washington.

At the White House Jacqueline got into a car with Bobby and Teddy and drove to the Capitol. They walked up the long steps, knelt at the coffin for a minute, took several steps back, then turned and went out. Behind them, eight pallbearers lifted the casket off the catafalque and carried it outside and down the stairs between sentinels representing all the armed services. The coffin slid onto the waiting caisson and was strapped down. The rear gate was closed.

In slow procession, the Kennedy family in cars followed the caisson back to the White House. Across the street, in Lafayette Square, thousands waited to watch the start of a procession that will probably never be repeated in American history. There was de Gaulle in his Khaki uniform and square cap of the French army, the small, slight Haile Selassie in beautiful braid; Prince Philip in the blue of the Royal Navy; many other dignitaries in hats, sashes, medals, or civilian clothes.

In the quiet stillness, one could hear the tolling of church bells. Flags, at half-mast, lifted and fell in the breeze.

Jackie emerged once again from the White House. She walked toward the caisson and took her place behind it. She wore a black coat and a long black veil. On her right, in morning coat, was Bobby; on her left, Teddy.

As the skirl of the Black Watch bagpipes began, the caisson moved off. The First Lady followed on foot. Next, on foot also, came President and Lady Bird Johnson, Steve Smith, Sargent Shriver, James Auchincloss, and the guards of the Secret Service. Following came a limousine bearing Caroline and John-John.

And walking behind them, in a large, somewhat disarrayed group that was nevertheless impressive in its splendor, came the great personages—de Gaulle, Erhardt, Mikoyan, Douglas-Home, Ikeda, Selassie, De Valera, Brandt. Next came the justices of the Supreme Court, the members of the Cabinet, and the close associates of Jack Kennedy.

The black caisson wheels glistened in the sunlight; the carriage trappings jangled as it went.

Jackie took Bobby's hand as they started up the street. Her brown hair and the majestic beauty of her sad face could be seen only when the wind lightly whipped the veil against her face. Then she let go of Bobby's hand and walked alone.

Millions throughout the world watched as she stepped along without faltering, her head straight forward, looking neither right nor left. A nation's earlier doubts about this woman's character, strength, and grace no longer existed.

The march, to the cadence of muffled drums, was six blocks long. The phalanx that followed behind the woman with lips that trembled and eyes that glistened walked six abreast, rivalries foregone. Some had argued with John Kennedy. Some had been enemies at times of his country; others had asked for his help. Now they dignified the sorrow by walking behind the President.

At last the cortege came to the old red church. Jacqueline waited a few moments for the children. She took them up the stairs, holding them by the hand. John-John was crying until distracted by Cardinal Cushing's bright vestments. The Cardinal put his arm around Jacqueline. She genuflected before him. He then leaned down and kissed Caroline and patted John-John. Jacqueline and the children went on into the cathedral; Cardinal Cushing waited outside for the casket.

The honor guard unbuckled the straps that held the casket to the caisson. "Hail to the Chief," played with ruffles and flourishes, came from the army band. The Cardinal descended the steps. The band played a dirge, and the color guard and

pallbearers carried the coffin to the waiting Cardinal. He blessed the coffin with holy water. He kissed the flag reverently as it was removed. The coffin was revealed as dark wood in the sunlight. The Cardinal, reading from his prayer book, led the procession up the stairs and into the church.

Jacqueline sat in the front pew with the children beside her. Bobby and Rose sat in the same row. Jacqueline was close enough to the coffin to reach out and touch it. In the second row were the men and women of the Kennedy family; in the third, Jacqueline's mother and relatives of the Auchincloss family.

Across the center aisle sat President Johnson and Lady Bird. Behind were former Presidents Eisenhower and Truman with Mamie and Margaret.

The Romanesque interior echoed with the start of the Low Mass, which is spoken rather than sung. Only Cardinal Cushing officiated, though two archbishops and four bishops sat in the sanctuary.

"Life is not taken away . . . life is but changed. . . .

"You are not to lament over them as the rest of the world does, with no hope to live by. We believe that as Jesus underwent death and rose again, so God will bring back all those who have found rest through Him. . . ."

Now the Cardinal offered communion. There was no sound or movement as Jacqueline went forward. She lifted her veil over her hat and stopped at the communion rail. Robert followed and knelt by her side as the Cardinal placed the consecrated host on their tongues. Other members of the family came forward. Then scores followed, perhaps two hundred in all. . . .

There was no eulogy. But when the Mass was ended, the Most Reverend Philip Hannan went to the high pulpit and read favorite biblical passages of President Kennedy and then, as requested by Jacqueline, his 1961 inaugural address with its famous challenge: "Ask not what your country can do for you; ask rather what you can do for your country."

Now Cardinal Cushing walked from the high altar to pronounce absolution over the mortal remains of the late President. As he circled the casket twice, sprinkling it with holy water and

At one o'clock, Jackie and the children come out onto the north portico of the White House. The horse-drawn caisson bearing Jack Kennedy's body then proceeded to the Capitol rotunda. The only sound on the crowded streets was the beat of muffled drums.

perfuming it with incense, the congregation recited the Lord's Prayer.

The cathedral choir chanted the Gregorian "In Paradisium" as the Cardinal moved down the aisle after a few words with Jackie and Caroline. Behind him came the pallbearers with the casket.

The President had been to his last Mass. Over his body his old friend and pastor had pronounced the words of comfort and terrible finality: *"Requiescat in pace . . ."* (May he rest in peace.)

The service was concluded. Jacqueline walked slowly out of the cathedral with Caroline and John-John. She passed rows of friends, many of whom could hardly control their sobs. As they reached the open light of day, Caroline began to sob uncontrollably. So too, did Jackie, the first time that day in public. Then she controlled herself and comforted her daughter. She would cry only once again in public, later at the Arlington gravesite.

At the bottom of the steps, there occurred a startling and heartrending incident. As the soldiers saluted his father in his casket, young John-John saluted, too, his left hand stiffly at his side, his right in correct position at his forehead. . . .

The ride to Arlington and the walk up the grassy hillside that lay between the Custis-Lee mansion and the Lincoln Memorial took over an hour.

"I could spend the rest of my life here," Jack Kennedy had said when he had stopped to visit on November 11, Armistice Day. Now they lifted him off the caisson for the very last time and placed him over the open earth. The American flag was held in place above the grave by the guards. The Irish regiment went through its silent ritual of arms. The bagpipes of the air force played their melancholy air. Overhead, roaring through the sky, came the jets. In salute they dipped over the site, followed by *Air Force One,* and a leaderless formation of planes, symbolic of the nation's loss.

The bugler sounded taps on the hill. There was a twenty-one-gun salute in three volleys by the riflemen. The honor guard folded the commemorative flag and handed it to Jacqueline. Cardinal Cushing pronounced the last funeral rites.

Then Jackie was given the torch to light the eternal flame. She handed it to Bobby, who touched the torch to the flames again, as did Teddy.

And so concluded the burial services of John Fitzgerald Kennedy, thirty-fifth President of the United States.

The Family
Draws Together

The role of patriarch fell to the third son. The family looked to Bobby. The large decisions, once made by Joe and after him, by Jack, now came to Bobby. The burden of leadership was now greater than ever.

Presidential families fade slowly from the public eye after the incumbent's term ends. The public looks to their successors and it turns back only occasionally, largely out of curiosity, to former Presidents' families. But curiosity diminishes as time passes.

For the Kennedy family, however, this was not true. Americans and this family were bound together in a common tragedy. Obscurity was not possible for the Kennedys as long as there were generations that had lived through tragedy with them.

But, to begin again as we must, the wife and children needed a new home. Jackie moved out of the White House on December 6, two weeks after Jack's funeral.

Heading for a Democratic caucus one day, Bobby and Teddy run into each other in the halls of the Senate.

She borrowed a home in Georgetown from Ambassador Averell Harriman, then three months later moved one block away on the same street, to a house she leased for a year. It was big enough for her family, and for the Secret Service men who were to stay with them for years.

Seven months later, having decided Washington carried too much of the past, Jackie went to New York. She bought a five-bedroom, fifteenth-floor apartment on the corner of Fifth Avenue and 85th Street, facing Central Park. She came to New York in time to put Caroline, age six, in the second grade at the Convent of the Sacred Heart School on East 91st Street. It was the same school that Pat's eight-year-old daughter, Sydney, attended. And in New York Jackie was close to Jean, who also had a small family (for a Kennedy) and was her city neighbor. Here she became a constant New York wonder to everyone in the city. Invariably they would stare, or look away, or follow her. Privacy was difficult.

Before Jackie left Washington, she, Teddy, and Bobby held a press conference in Bobby's office in the Justice Department to thank the 800,000 Americans who had sent her letters of condolence. They would be placed, she said, in the John F. Kennedy Memorial Library to be built in Boston with funds donated by the public. By year's end, the library received $10 million in American contributions.

Rose traveled for the library fund-raising, with a JFK memorial exhibit. It contained photographs, drafts of famous speeches, and mementos such as the coconut shell on which Jack had scratched the *PT-109* rescue message. The display often coincided with ceremonies renaming streets, parks, plazas, or buildings in memory of John F. Kennedy.

Jackie's return to New York came before Bobby's resignation as attorney general. After he resigned, he also went to live in New York. He left Washington because he realized that Lyndon Johnson would not want him on the ticket as vice-president in the next election. Bobby must run for office on his own. The way to reach his true ambition in time, the Presidency, was to start in the Senate, as Jack had done. And in New York he could run for office against a Republican incumbent. The state had one of the largest delegate votes at the Democratic conventions, where Presidents are nominated.

Bobby moved to a big, rambling house on Glen Cove, Long Island, and also kept an apartment in Manhattan. He announced in August that he would run against Republican Kenneth Keating, the incumbent, for the Senate.

An accident, and near tragedy occurred on June 19. Ted was doing some campaign work, flying around in a rented plane. It crashed into an apple orchard not far from Springfield, Massachusetts. The pilot and a friend of Ted's in his employ, Edward Moss, were killed. Birch Bayh, the Indiana senator, and his wife escaped injury.

Teddy, who had been half standing in the middle of the plane at the time of the crash, was dragged out of the wreckage. Surgeons discovered three vertebrae in his lower back smashed, two ribs cracked, and blood surrounding his spleen and left kidney. The condition of the third lumbar was precarious. It had been driven so far sideways that it almost snapped the cord. Another half inch would have left him paralyzed.

Bobby and Joan discovered him in the hospital in an oxygen tent "with tubes up his nose, things dangling from both arms," as Joan described it. He managed a very weak, "Hi, Joansie."

The next six months were spent recovering in the hospital, mostly in traction, strapped horizontal to a rotating Stryker frame. Time in repose brought about a change in Teddy. A certain detachment that he never had before set in. He took on a more mature attitude, one that resembled Jack's, even to the speech pattern.

Bobby's winning campaign for the New York Senate seat started. Ethel was out working for him. So was Rose, now in her middle seventies, who had sworn she would never campaign again. But she came to New York to help her son. She hadn't lost her humor. Asked why she had first refused to help Bobby, she said, "He knows." Bobby confessed it was because he never picked up his clothes when he was a kid. Her fiftieth wedding anniversary was spent in Newburgh, New York, stumping through the Italian district.

Bobby won his Senate seat, as everyone predicted he would. He moved with Ethel and their ten children back to Hickory Hill, just outside Washington, D.C., and joined Teddy in the Senate.

For the seven families, the five years after the President's assassination were spent much like the old days—politics, family gatherings, public and business pursuits, helping twenty-plus children grow up. The Kennedy years were being replaced in America. The country's atmosphere had changed drastically. By 1967, the nation was deep in the Vietnam quagmire. Opposition came to Lyndon Johnson, elected in 1964 over Barry Goldwater, from college campuses as students rose up against the war. The youth revolution was in full swing. The black civil rights movement was growing stronger.

Bobby had broken with LBJ on Vietnam in 1966. By 1967, he had spoken out, asking for a halt in bombing and a truce to be administered by the UN. "It is we who lived in abundance and sent out young men to die. It is our chemicals that scorch children and our bombs which level villages."

By mid-1967, friends and advisers wanted Bobby to run against Lyndon Johnson for the presidential nomination. A year previous, a national poll indicated that people preferred Bobby to Johnson as the next Democratic candidate. In the five years since Jack's death, Bobby Kennedy had become the most popular man in the nation.

But Bobby couldn't actively campaign against Johnson. To do so would immediately, and openly, split the party. The Republicans, though weaker, could exploit this and elect Richard Nixon. Nevertheless, Bobby's reluctance to battle

Two months after the assassination, Jackie makes her first appearance on TV to thank the eight hundred thousand people who wrote her letters of condolence. To give her moral support she chose to appear with Bobby and Teddy in Bobby's Justice Department office.

Jackie and Bobby, who had taken over the family leadership, hold a brief press conference in New York to help raise funds for the John F. Kennedy Memorial Library and to advertise an exhibit of the late President's papers and memorabilia.

On his first day in the Senate, in January 1965, Bobby is taken around by Teddy and introduced to members. It had been 160 years since brothers served together in the Senate.

At New England Baptist Hospital a few days before Christmas 1964, Teddy takes his first steps after months of convalescing from a near-fatal plane crash. His father, crippled by a stroke in 1961, rose to his feet to visit and encourage his son.

Johnson confused people. Meanwhile, Eugene McCarthy, a Democratic senator from Minnesota, went after Johnson. He and his following of young college students worked hard in the New Hampshire primary to defeat the President.

When the Tet offensive, a massive attack by the North Vietnamese, came in January 1968, it showed plainly that America was not winning in Vietnam as the Pentagon had claimed. It meant the war would go on longer and not close by year's end. Johnson's veracity was undermined. New polls again showed that Bobby would do well in a primary runoff against Johnson, which would lead to the Democratic nomination for President. Still, Bobby waited.

At this point several important events occurred in close sequence. The Kerner Report, an investigation of the causes of black riots in the cities, showed that the problem was due to white racism. White racism and black civil rights became a campaign issue that Bobby could pursue, but Lyndon Johnson could not. Johnson had worked hard on civil rights. He had done comparatively well. But he wasn't going any further. So he was politically vulnerable both domestically and in foreign affairs.

Senator McCarthy took New Hampshire from Johnson by a huge margin. He won twenty of the twenty-four precincts, cutting into LBJ's try for a second nomination to the Presidency. Two days after McCarthy's win, Bobby announced that he would run in the primaries. The spot he chose for the announcement was the Senate room where Jack had once announced his candidacy. Many said that Bobby was riding on McCarthy's coattails. It was somewhat true, and Bobby could only ignore the criticism.

Bobby organized a highly experienced campaign staff. Most of the team, including Ted Sorensen, had worked for all three Kennedy brothers in politics. Bobby was a seasoned campaigner by now. And the public response to his campaign was explosive. Crowds moved in and pulled at him; they shouted out his name. An underlying Kennedy adoration was coming out.

On the night of March 31, the campaign was left wide open to all candidates. Lyndon Johnson announced on television that he would not seek the nomination for President.

On April 4, 1968, Dr. Martin Luther King, Jr., was assassinated in a Memphis motel by James Earl Ray. The reaction in black America was volatile. Cities were set afire and riots erupted.

The "black issues" in America—ghettos, civil rights, racism, and oppression—were as important as Vietnam. Despite Bobby's wealth and privileged upbringing, blacks believed in him; they felt he would do something about racism if elected. Minorities would vote for him. So would whites, who thought he could help solve the black problem. Minority problems were his issue.

Bobby won handily in Indiana, beating McCarthy and Hubert Humphrey (who would eventually be the Democratic candidate that year, and lose to Richard Nixon). Bobby won again, and soundly, in Nebraska. But in Oregon he lost to McCarthy by

Baby Patrick Joseph takes a bow four days after his birth. His parents emerge from Boston's St. Elizabeth's Hospital with their third child on July 18, 1967.

Uncle Ted, surrogate father to John Jr., totes his nephew piggyback in a canvas carrier down a ski run at Stowe, Vermont. Both Kennedy families gathered there for an Easter weekend in 1967.

Bobby, in checked shorts, leads a large party of family and friends in four rubber rafts on a trip down the Colorado River. The group spent four days traveling eighty miles down the Grand Canyon.

Bobby lugs barefoot, eight-year-old Kerry over the rocky road during a trip down the Colorado River. Ethel takes care of the family cat that went along on the trip.

Right: A very relieved Bobby greets Ethel who had followed him down the freezing Hudson River in her kayak. She tipped over three times before reaching home point. Bobby wears a leather jacket inherited from Jack.

A crowd has gathered to watch Bobby ski to the bottom of a slope at Tupper Lake in the Adirondack Mountains. He attracted young people wherever he went, and in the Senate he was dubbed the senator of the young.

Taking a turn on the ice around New York's Rockefeller Center rink, Bobby and a sportily clad Ethel give a skating party for his hard-working staff and their friends. The two hundred people enjoyed oyster patties, hot chestnuts, and mulled wine.

Bobby visits a South American town, Villa Dulce, in Chile, where students and parents dedicate a new school named for John F. Kennedy. The adoration of the martyred President was shared in many parts of the world.

An annual children's party at the Kennedy home in MacLean, Virginia, for the foreign diplomats' offspring finds Bobby "wearing" a mass of balloons while he welcomes the guests.

Senator Kennedy, lighting up during a hearing in the Senate, has let his hair grow out in the style of the young.

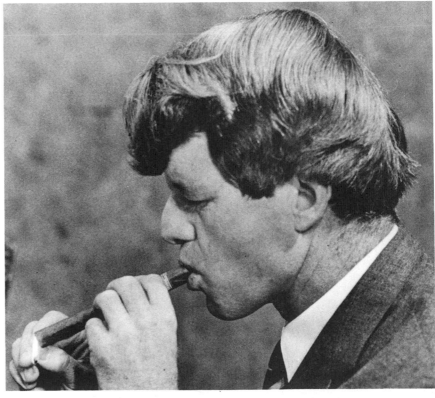

Right: *Eager hands reach out to Bobby during the presidential primary campaign in Sacramento. All over the country people wanted to shake his hand.*

Jackie, dressed in a mod 1969 outfit, pauses on a Manhattan corner before crossing the street on a warm September afternoon. She had become a New York attraction, one of the celebrities whom visitors hoped to see.

After lunch on a stroll outside New York's Plaza Hotel, Jackie leads the two men in her life: John Jr., in natty scarf and blazer, holds a discussion with Aristotle Onassis, his step-father of four months.

Jackie and Caroline, aged nine, test the snow before starting a run at the famous ski resort at Sun Valley, Idaho in 1966.

A beaming Bobby Kennedy on the night of June 5, 1968, accepts the victory cheers from the jammed-in crowd in the Ambassador Hotel ballroom. "On to Chicago," he said, as he left the podium by way of the kitchen where Sirhan Sirhan was waiting to assassinate him.

six points. He was depressed not only because this was his first solid political defeat but also because his future was at stake. Everything now turned on the outcome of the next primary—the one in California. California had a huge voting delegation to the convention. If Bobby won, taking the convention was almost a foregone conclusion. If he did not, he was in deep political trouble.

A debate between McCarthy and Bobby, expected to be a high point, a clash of giants, went on KGO-TV in San Francisco. It turned out to be a tepid meeting, though viewers felt Bobby won. Bobby campaigned his way down to Los Angeles in the last days before the primary. The results would be waited out at the Ambassador Hotel. On the night of June 5, 1968, he seemed to be losing, but

the networks declared him the winner in California. He was upstairs in his hotel room when the announcement came. He went down in the elevator with Ethel to a jammed ballroom to talk with the celebrating people. Before hundreds of cheering friends and workers in the Embassy Room, he thanked everyone. "Now it's on to Chicago—and let's win there!"

Bobby stepped down from the podium, with Ethel following him. He made his way through the hotel kitchen, where Sirhan Sirhan was waiting for him with a gun.

Bobby Kennedy had once said, "I play Russian roulette every time I get up in the morning. I just don't care. There's nothing I can do about it anyway." He meant he was a helpless target for any would-be assassin determined to kill him.

He was taken by ambulance, still alive, to Good Samaritan Hospital in Los Angeles. By the time Teddy, finished with campaigning and waiting in San Francisco, got to Los Angeles, Bobby was not expected to live. Teddy sat up half of Thursday night. He would go back to New York with Bobby's body, Ethel, and Jackie, then travel to Hyannis to

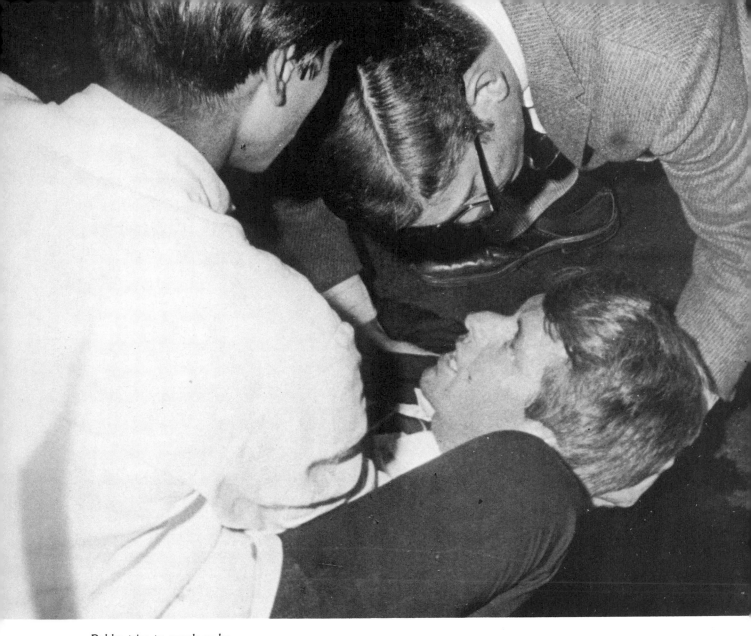

Bobby tries to speak as he lies wounded on the kitchen floor of the Ambassador Hotel in Los Angeles. He was shot in the head by Sirhan Sirhan moments after making his victory speech to the ballroom crowd.

Ethel kneels beside the mortally wounded Bobby in the kitchen of the Ambassador Hotel. A rosary rests under his inert fingers.

Right: Ethel, wearing a dark, transparent veil mourns for Bobby at St. Patrick's Cathedral in New York City. He was eulogized by Teddy.

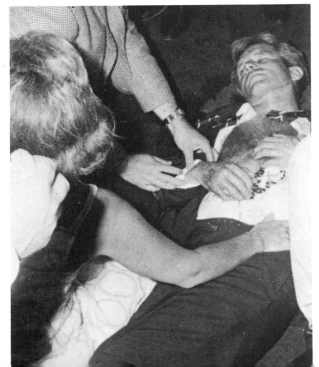

tell Joe about the death of still another of his sons.

On Thursday, June 6, press officer Frank Mankiewicz, looking haggard and worn, announced at the hospital that Bobby Kennedy was dead. Two hours later, Pierre Salinger, Jack's former press officer, revealed specifics of the funeral arrangements.

The body of the forty-three-year-old senator would be flown on a plane dispatched by the White House for a Requiem Mass at St. Patrick's Cathedral in New York. A train would then journey to Washington, D.C., with the body and mourners. Bobby would be buried in Arlington National Cemetery, near Jack.

The autopsy took six hours and delayed the White House jet's takeoff. Jackie arrived in Los Angeles just before the flight. The body was brought to the airport, the coffin was put on a fork lift and placed on the plane.

The flight to New York took four and one-half hours. Halfway out, Jackie wanted to get off. She thought this was the same plane that had carried Jack from Dallas to Washington. She was assured it was not, that it was another White House jet, one that had been on its way to Tokyo at the time of the shooting.

Ethel, Jackie, and Teddy kept to themselves in the forward cabin with the coffin draped in a maroon cloth. They were weary and hadn't slept. Both Ethel and Teddy fell asleep beside the coffin.

Waiting for the funeral plane when it landed at La Guardia Airport in New York were Joan Kennedy and Eunice and Sargent Shriver. The airport was very quiet. It was hot and full of despair, sorrow, and weeping. The big plane taxied to a stop at two minutes before nine in the evening, directly in front of the waiting group on the tarmac. Joan and Sargent moved onto a hoist that carried them up to the front exit.

Newsmen, photographers, and the crowd struggled to get closer. Thursday's arrival was the only disorderly moment in the next three days, which ended in Washington, D.C.—except for a shocking tragedy. Near Baltimore, two people in the crowd that lined the path of the funeral train from New York to Washington were killed when they stepped on the track.

At the airport a cortege was formed. A gray Cadillac hearse with Ethel and Teddy in the front seat, and the body in back, led a thirty-four car procession slowly to the center of New York City.

Rose was waiting outside the cathedral in a car.

After the body arrived at St. Patrick's, some two hundred waiting friends attended a short service. The coffin was on a bier at the front of the cathedral, between the rows of seats. Afterward, Ethel and Jackie went to stay at the Carlyle Hotel. Robert McNamara, who had overall charge of the funeral arrangements, brought Ethel photographs of the gravesite in Washington for her approval.

Steve Smith and Teddy held a meeting with the planners of the funeral rites. They insisted that anything military be kept in the background. Because Bobby had been in opposition to the war in Vietnam, trumpets and drums would be a contradiction. Nor did they want to compete with the grand flourishes at John's funeral. But Bobby had been in the navy. And he was being buried at Arlington, a military cemetery. So there could be a navy pallbearer group in reserve. And a navy band could play the "Navy Hymn" when the coffin was taken from the train in Washington. But at the gravesite, civilians would carry the coffin to the grave.

Arrangements had to be made, too, for the cathedral seating. Hundreds from the press and the United Nations, plus dignitaries and political officials, wanted to be present.

After the cathedral ceremony a wake was held. Almost all of the Kennedy family attended. It was an Irish wake, which meant a gathering of people who saw tragedy very often and grappled with it in their way. They laughed and sang and joked. Those present who were not Irish were offended.

Eight Masses were said during the next day, the public mourning day. Lines formed around the church—to Park Avenue, down to 45th Street, up Park Avenue on the other side of the street, and back to the church on 50th Street. In the crowds were blacks, "ethnics," the poor and not so poor, the young and not so young. The church was supposed to close that night in preparation for the next day's funeral. But the lines were long, and the cathedral remained open until five in the morning. At the funeral, Ethel sat in the front row with Rose. All ten of Ethel and Bobby's children were present. So were all their nieces and nephews. Ethel watched as her three oldest boys—Joe, Robert, and David—wearing white suplices, served as altar boys. As the ceremony went on, Jackie wept. She and Bobby had been very close. He had become her close support and mentor since Jack's death.

Rose lowered her head slowly several times and closed her eyes. She was now seventy-eight and was doing what no parent should do, burying her child.

Teddy read the eulogy.

We loved him as a brother, and as a father and as a son. From his parents and from his older brothers and sisters, Joe and Kathleen and Jack, he received inspiration. . . . He gave us strength in time of trouble, wisdom in time of uncertainty, and sharing in time of happiness. . . . My brother need not be idealized, or enlarged in death beyond what he was in life, to be remembered simply as a good and decent man, who saw wrong and tried to right it, saw suffering and tried to heal it, saw war and tried to stop it. . . . Some men see things as they are and say "why?" I dream things that never were and say "why not?"

What Robert Kennedy might have accomplished in a normal lifespan is unknown. But, if he had become President, we would have had no Watergate, and the extraordinary mistrust of politicians today might not have come. The war in Vietnam might have ended sooner, and some young Americans who died in that war would be living today.

Late that afternoon, the train carrying Bobby's body and his grieving family left Pennsylvania Station for Washington, D.C. People on the train were startled to find Ethel and Joe III coming through the cars, thanking people for their expression of concern.

It was night when the train arrived in Washington. The casket was taken from Union Station to Arlington. Mourners followed in groups, carrying candles. The ceremony was simple and almost informal. Robert Kennedy was buried on a small, grassy hill.

Afterward, Rose, leaving the site, stumbled on the dark hill. Then, regaining her step and poise, clutching a single white candle, she walked among her grandchildren to a waiting car.

Joe's condition deteriorated following Bobby's death. Near the end, at age eighty-one, he could not feed himself and had to suffer the annoyances and indignities of the helpless. By sheer will he hung on until November 18, 1969. Then, surrounded by his family, he passed away.

"I was kneeling by his bedside," said Rose,

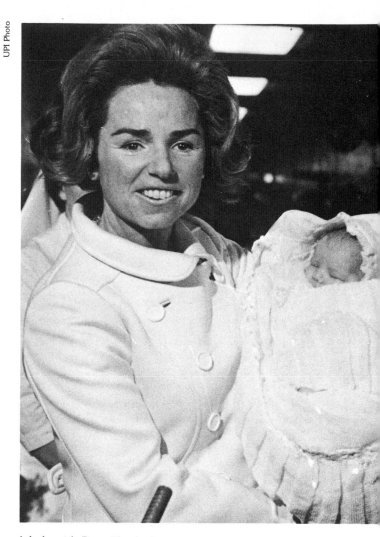

A baby girl, Rory Elizabeth Katherine, was born to Ethel in Washington, D.C., after Bobby's death. The infant's arrival, six months after the assassination, reminds us that life will be renewed.

"holding his hand. Next to Almighty God, I had loved him—do love him—with all my heart, all my soul, all my mind."

Six months after Bobby's death, on December 12, 1968, Ethel Kennedy gave birth to a daughter. A month later the child was christened by Archbishop Terence Cooke, who came down from New York to St. Luke's Catholic Church in MacLean, Virginia. The baby was held by her eleven-year-old sister, Mary; standing at Mary's side was her brother Michael, age twelve. The brother and sister were godparents to the infant, christened Rory Catherine Elizabeth Kennedy, eleventh child of Robert and Ethel. Rory was the last of twenty-seven born of the fifth generation since Patrick Kennedy from Ireland crossed the Atlantic on a packet boat, to arrive in America in 1848.

The Inheritors

One September night in 1976, Rose Kennedy's home was inundated by thirty Kennedys, Lawfords, Shrivers, and Smiths. They came to her house in Hyannis Port to celebrate the eighty-fifth birthday of the unsinkable Founding Mother, as she is sometimes called. The children brought her a leather-bound book, seven months in the making, a gift that contained an original poem or essay by each and all the family.

It included an apt, witty tribute. Addressing the Founding Mother as "our grammar instructor and favorite linguist," because she liked to correct their language, she was described as "the great golfer and consummate swimmer, our movie operator and manners authority, Florida proprietor and midnight dancer, Parisian swinger and general leader." It was a sentimental book, but tempered with Kennedy humor and bite. "She is slight and beautiful, yet her granddaughters have thunder

John and Caroline, who both inherited the handsome features of their mom and dad, follow a match at the Robert F. Kennedy tennis benefit for underprivileged children in New York. Fifteen years had passed since they played in the Oval Office.

thighs and boulder bottoms. Thanks a lot, Grandma!" wrote her granddaughters in a genetic complaint.

The party was postponed from July, her birthday month, to September because, as the fifth generation grows older and leaves home, it becomes more difficult to gather them under one roof from various parts of the world. But the effort was worth it. They had a glorious time.

Missing from Rose's party was Kathleen Kennedy Townsend, Bobby and Ethel's oldest, who lives in Santa Fe, New Mexico, with her professor husband, David, and their year-old daughter, Meagan Ann Kennedy Townsend. The child is number one in the sixth generation of American Kennedys.

If this genealogical review of Kennedy growth makes those feel ancient who can remember clearly where they were on the day the President died, consider John F. Kennedy if he had lived and attended this party for his mother. He would be sixty, quite possibly a balding patriarch, wearing glasses, who had gone back to the Senate after his years as President were up.

Granchildren grow up. Joe Kennedy III, Ethel's oldest son, is the first to turn to politics. Numerous Kennedy grandchildren have helped in political campaigns. Maria and Timothy Shriver campaigned for their father, Sarge, when he ran as vice-presidential candidate with George McGovern against Nixon in 1972. But it is Joe who, after an uncertain start and some time spent wandering over several continents (not unlike his Uncle Jack, who tried journalism before running for Congress), has chosen politics full time. Perhaps there is something toprenatal influence. Joe was born just after Ethel returned from a hectic day of campaigning in Fall River, Massachusetts, for Jack's try for the Senate after three terms as congressman.

In 1976, Ted made Joe III manager of his reelection campaign to the Senate. He earned his spurs, campaigning in the streets, if not quite the title. Recently he purchased a residence in Boston, and is expected to enter the race for Congress. He will become the fourth generation of Kennedys to enter politics.

The Kennedy intellectual is Joe's younger brother, Robert Jr., twenty-three, an omnivorous reader and Harvard graduate who is preparing a book adapted from his doctoral thesis on the noted jurist Frank M. Johnson, whose work and rulings in federal court brought integration to Alabama.

Another talent at work is Robert Shriver, twenty-four, Eunice's oldest son who is a feature writer for the *Los Angeles Times*. After politics, writing is the chief enterprise in the Kennedy family.

No one doubts it is harder today than ever before to grow up a Kennedy. While their parents had attention paid to them as kids in England, there was never daily pursuit for gossip by the press and weekly sheets. This constant attention means that more is expected of a Kennedy today; they are hardly permitted to be young. A ticket for speeding becomes a national story on television.

"There were a lot of times," says Joe, who now accepts the attention as part of the territory, "when I didn't want to be in the public eye, when I felt my privacy was invaded when I'm not working and not intentionally putting myself in the public eye."

For years Caroline Kennedy, now a Radcliffe student, had stories made up about her because she was, as they say, the darling of the tabloids. A cold was pneumonia, gastritis was cancer, a date was sex, and a family quarrel was a battle. They liked pitting her against the most important cover star in America, her mother.

Her brother John, now a student at Andover, is old enough to become the subject of fantasies. He is dumb, smart, a showoff, a shy lad, clever, obtuse. One can take a choice.

Theories of the assassinations grow more bizarre, convoluted, and unsettling as time passes. They jab at a family wound that won't heal.

"I know," says Joe, "there are people writing that [the assassinations should be reopened]. I find it hard to read what's being written. There are apparently questions about the motives of the assassins. But, no matter what new investigations are started, they will never bring back my father or uncle. I'm satisfied they've found the individuals who pulled the triggers."

One by one, the parents' homes empty. The Shriver, Kennedy, Smith, and Lawford children go away to school or travel on their own. It leaves a void in the parents' lives that needs filling.

Caroline and John are away. Jackie's second husband, Aristotle Onassis, died in Paris on March 16, 1975, and was buried on Skorpios, his private island. Jackie decided to get a job. A friend, the publisher of The Viking Press, made her a working editor at a modest salary of $10,000 a year.

On her first day at work sidewalks outside the Madison Avenue offices of The Viking Press were jammed with reporters, photographers, TV news cameras, and ordinary rubbernecks when she arrived. It took awhile, but the editorial staff did get used to seeing her in the office and enjoyed working with her. She has since left Viking to work for another publisher, Doubleday. But the mail she receives continues: requests for a lock of her hair or an autographed photo, marriage offers, or manuscripts sent to her with new theories of the assassination.

Of course, the younger Kennedy children are still at home. Ethel has four of her eleven children living with her. Jean has two nine-year-old adopted daughters; Amanda, and Kym Maria, a Vietnamese girl. Pat's Robin is her only one at home. Eunice, who works almost full-time for the Kennedy Foundation for the retarded, has Robert and Timothy.

Joan is separate and special. The Kennedy ordeals have been particularly hard on her. She has had an alcohol problem. She has felt the need to go into therapy. She has endured the divorce of her parents, ending thirty-five years of marriage, and the death of her mother. She has survived Chappaquiddick, the scandal that nearly canceled Teddy out of public life. And she has suffered

Jean, Teddy, and Pat, in a glow of Kennedy vitality, enjoy a party in New York honoring noted philanthropist Mary Lasker.

Ted gives Joe III, who wants to get into congressional politics, a couple of tips on handling political fence-mending during a town celebration at Lowell, Massachusetts.

An exhausted Chris Lawford (rear), twenty-three, and his teammate-cousin Joe Kennedy cross the finish line in a twelve-mile canoe race on the Westfield River in Huntington, Massachusetts.

With good humor Teddy parries the inevitable question by a newsman from the floor of the Washington Press Club: Will he run for President? His answer is no, but, the press will only believe him if he says yes.

Teddy Jr., working in a traditional young man's summer job for $2.35 a hour, directs cars on the Nantucket-Hyannis ferry. The loss of his right leg is no handicap.

A contemplative Joan Kennedy waits for her husband to finish an interview in Stockholm, Sweden. She has recently confessed to personal problems, ending years of rumor and showing a Kennedy strength of character people have come to expect.

Led by Teddy, the gang huddles up to make plans for a big family ski weekend in New Hampshire. Today Ted is considered to be "the last Kennedy." Joe III is in back; Jean Smith, in knit cap and bangs, smiles; Teddy is on the right; and Joan brings up the rear.

The Kennedy party, adults and children on a visit to China, view Shanghai from the top of the Shanghai Mansion. The Kennedy families believe that regular foreign travel is a necessity in learning about oneself, the world, and others.

*At Falmouth on Cape Cod Joe III and Grandma work the old
Kennedy campaign trail together for Teddy's reelection. Grandma
thinks Joe will gather more votes if he cuts his hair shorter.*

*Robert Kennedy, Jr., holds a jackal
hawk while working on a special
television film in Kenya. His first book,
a journalist's report on Frank
Johnson, a federal judge who
successfully fought racial segregation,
was published in 1978.*

Ethel, the independent sailor, handles the foresail alone, helping to bring the family boat, Curragh, into the wind. She remains the family's leading outdoor athlete.

It is a proud occasion for Mom, on crutches as the result of a skiing accident. She joins nineteen-year-old David at graduation ceremonies at Middlesex School in Concord, Massachusetts.

A presidential primary rally in Chester, Pennsylvania finds Kathleen, Ethel's eldest daughter, on the campaign trail with George McGovern, who ran against Nixon in 1972.

Teddy Jr.'s cancer at age thirteen, and the subsequent amputation of his right leg.

Teddy, sometimes called the last Kennedy, is the most popular political figure in America today, according to the polls. He is expected to run for the Presidency one day. But, standing in the path to the White House is the riddle called Chappaquiddick.

Sometime during the night of July 18, 1969, Mary Jo Kopechne, twenty-eight, died in a 1967 Oldsmobile that was driven off a small bridge at Chappaquiddick Island. What would seem to be the most common of auto tragedies became one involving questions of morality. Ted Kennedy admitted driving the car. But his actions that night, as he has explained them, remain puzzling. Describing his motives on national television, he asked the public to vote for or against his remaining in office. They voted for him by a good margin. In a sense the vote forgave him, but it did not absolve him of his moral responsibility.

Because Chappaquiddick remains a scandal waiting to be revived by his opponents if he announces for the Presidency, and because a presidential term is believed to carry an enormous risk to his life (some feel he would never live out eight years in the White House) and because his wife, Joan, would be vulnerable emotionally under the exceptional stress of becoming First Lady, there are just as many people in Washington who expect Teddy will not run for the Presidency as those who do.

But there is more to be said on the matter. We know calamity sometimes changes people for the better. The crisis of Chappaquiddick, it's now believed by many, has turned Ted Kennedy into a better senator. He is said to be superior to his brothers, Jack and Bobby, in their own time. While he has lost some moral persuasion, he has taken the lead in public matters where other senators lacked political courage. On reflection, Richard Reeves, a noted and astute political writer, has said, "Edward Kennedy may be the best of the Kennedys. . . ."

The Kennedy-Fitzgerald clan, the fifth generation in America since 1849, gather around Rose (center), the Founding Mother, in her living room for a historic photo.

The Founding Mother steps up to receive an honorary degree from Georgetown University in Washington, D.C.

Recently, all the wives except Ethel, plus Teddy, Caroline, and three other children went to visit China together.

This is a different world for the coming Kennedy generations to meet than the one their parents knew. It's different, but what is to be retained from the past?

There is tradition. The twenty-nine grandchildren are among the privileged in America, as were their parents and grandparents. Their family tradition requires men and women not to squander their talents or their wealth. They are to be used to do good, to help the poor, the underprivileged, and the oppressed.

Rose has said that she hopes they will all remember where they came from, the Irish poverty and oppression, and how in a short time a family was formed in America that many in the world came to admire. Never forget gratitude, pride, and the obligation to improve this country.

The lesson in all that has happened to the Kennedys, she has said, is to keep faith, to find the strength to bear grief and disappointment with dignity and without self-pity.

And we admire that faith. The Kennedy family, because it is a presidential family, is our family, too. They come to us as an inheritance of our American history.

As contemporaries we live together, adding our own memories and personal feelings to those we see reflected in their lives from day to day.

But, there is more to be said. The Kennedy family also reflects and speaks of American events that go back for a hundred and fifty years. It symbolizes all immigrant families that have come to America and risen. The family success is probably as much as we honestly can expect of the American dream in the way of fulfillment. So they remain in our thoughts as a family greater than, in fact, they are.

One cannot, therefore, escape the sense that our lives and theirs are bound together. Where they go and what they do always unconsciously speak to us. Obviously, this becomes a special responsibility for the Kennedys.

Now we are passing through a period of revision as happens when time moves on and we change. We look back with open eyes. Though we can find faults and weaknesses in the people, what cannot be denied are the qualities we have always sensed in the family: that which is good and loving, a certain glory and, above all, the expression of group strength that helps them endure, as it does in all families.

Index